# Mediterranean Diet For Beginners

## The Complete Guide to Get Started With The Top 10 Tips to Success

+

## 110 Delicious Recipes and 14-Day Diet Meal Plan

*Includes Essential Principles for Weight Loss with Foods to Eat + Foods to Avoid*

**MARK WILLIAM**

Copyright © 2019 Mark William

All rights reserved.

All rights reserved. No part of this guide may be reproduced in any form without permission in writing from the publisher except in the case of brief quotations embodied in critical articles or reviews.

Legal & Disclaimer

The information contained in this book and its contents is not designed to replace or take the place of any form of medical or professional advice; and is not meant to replace the need for independent medical, financial, legal or other professional advice or services, as may be required. The content and information in this book have been provided for educational and entertainment purposes only.

The content and information contained in this book have been compiled from sources deemed reliable, and it is accurate to the best of the Author's knowledge, information, and belief. However, the Author cannot guarantee its accuracy and validity and cannot be held liable for any errors and/or omissions. Further, changes are periodically made to this book as and when needed. Where appropriate and/or necessary, you must consult a professional (including but not limited to your doctor, attorney, financial advisor or such other professional advisor) before using any of the suggested remedies, techniques or information in this book.

Upon using the contents and information contained in this book, you agree to hold harmless the Author from and against any damages, costs, and expenses, including any legal fees potentially resulting from the application of any of the information provided by this book. This disclaimer applies to any loss, damages or injury caused by the use and application

whether directly or indirectly, of any advice or information presented, whether for breach of contract, tort, negligence, personal injury, criminal intent, or under any other cause of action.

You agree to accept all risks of using the information presented inside this book.

You agree that by continuing to read this book, where appropriate and/or necessary, you shall consult a professional (including but not limited to your doctor, attorney, or financial advisor or such other advisor as needed) before using any of the suggested remedies, techniques, or information in this book.

**Table of Contents**

Introduction of Mediterranean Diet................................ 10

Chapter-1: Understanding the Mediterranean Diet......... 10

    The History of the Mediterranean Diet....................... 10

    What is the Mediterranean Diet?................................. 11

    Description of the Mediterranean Diet: ..................... 13

    Benefits of the Mediterranean Diet............................. 15

Chapter-2: Starting the Mediterranean Diet.................... 17

    Planning the Mediterranean Diet ................................ 17

    Precautions:................................................................... 17

    The Top 10 Tips to Success......................................... 18

Chapter-3: Foods to Eat .................................................. 20

Chapter-4: Foods to Avoid .............................................. 23

Chapter 5: What is the       Mediterranean Diet Pyramid?
................................................................................... 24

    How to utilize the Mediterranean Diet Plan for effective weight loss? .............................................................. 25

Breakfast Recipes............................................................. 30

    Date & Yogurt Smoothie............................................. 30

    Blueberry & Banana Smoothie.................................... 31

    Mixed Fruit Smoothie.................................................. 31

## Mediterranean Diet For Beginners

Green Fruity Smoothie ................................................. 32

Strawberry Smoothie Bowl .......................................... 33

Yogurt Bowl with Caramelized Figs ............................ 34

Yogurt & Pomegranate Bowl ....................................... 35

Avocado Toast .............................................................. 35

Smoked Salmon Toast .................................................. 36

Tahini & Feta Toast ...................................................... 38

Honeyed Ricotta & Peach Toast .................................. 38

Breakfast Sandwich ...................................................... 40

Couscous with Dried Fruit ........................................... 41

Barley with Warm Berry Compote .............................. 42

Spiced Quinoa Porridge ............................................... 43

Fruity Quinoa Bowl ...................................................... 45

Overnight Quinoa with Dried Fruit ............................ 46

Spiced Quinoa & Banana Bake .................................... 47

Overnight Fruity Oatmeal ........................................... 48

Overnight Oatmeal with Figs ...................................... 49

Oatmeal & Yogurt Bowl ............................................... 50

Strawberry & Yogurt Muffins ...................................... 51

Nutty & Fruity Oat Muffins ......................................... 53

Quinoa & Veggie Muffins ............................................. 55

Cheesy Veggie Muffins ................................................. 56

Baked Yogurt Crepes .................................................... 57

Eggs in Tomato Cups ................................................. 59

Oat Pancakes ............................................................. 60

Eggs in Spicy Veggie Sauce ....................................... 61

Eggs in Tomato Sauce ............................................... 63

Eggs with Avocado .................................................... 64

Tomato Omelet ......................................................... 65

Veggie Omelet ........................................................... 66

Veggies & Egg Scramble ........................................... 67

Veggies & Chickpeas Hash ....................................... 68

Spinach Frittata ......................................................... 69

Zucchini Frittata ....................................................... 70

Lunch Recipes ............................................................... 72

Tabbouleh ................................................................. 72

Cauliflower & Farro Salad ........................................ 73

Quinoa & Veggies Salad ........................................... 74

Chickpeas, Beans & Veggie Salad ............................ 76

Asparagus, Arugula & Pasta Salad ........................... 77

Orzo & Veggie Salad ................................................ 78

Tuna, Beans & Veggies Salad ................................... 79

Veggie Tortilla Wraps ............................................... 81

Lamb Filled Pita with Yogurt Sauce ........................ 82

Grilled Veggie Sandwiches ....................................... 83

Chicken Sandwiches with Aiolo .............................. 84

## Mediterranean Diet For Beginners

Ham & Veggies Sandwich ............................................. 86

Pita Pizza with Zucchini ............................................... 88

Pita Pizza with Shrimp ................................................. 89

Chicken & Veggies Flatbread Pizza ............................. 90

Mixed Veggies Pizza ..................................................... 91

Beef & Veggie Pizza ...................................................... 92

Falafel with Tahini Sauce ............................................. 94

Lamb Koftas with Yogurt Sauce .................................. 96

Chickpeas & Veggie Gazpacho .................................... 97

Spicy Tomato Soup ....................................................... 98

Zucchini & Basil Soup ................................................ 100

Veggies Soup .............................................................. 101

Chickpeas Stew ........................................................... 102

Vegetable Curry .......................................................... 103

Couscous with Cauliflower & Dates .......................... 105

Chicken & Veggie Kabobs .......................................... 107

Chicken & Grape Kebabs ........................................... 108

Grilled Prawns with Garlic Sauce .............................. 110

Octopus in Honey Sauce ............................................ 111

Mussels in Wine & Tomato Sauce ............................. 113

Pasta with Tomatoes & Herbs ................................... 114

Pasta with Mushrooms ............................................... 115

Pasta with Veggies ...................................................... 116

Pasta with Shrimp & Spinach .................................. 118

Rigatoni with Salmon ............................................... 119

Dinner Recipes ............................................................ 121

Spicy Lentil Soup ...................................................... 121

Chicken & Pasta Soup .............................................. 122

Lamb, Lentils & Chickpeas Soup ............................. 124

Cannellini Beans & Farro Stew ................................ 125

Quinoa, Beans and Vegetables Stew ........................ 127

Beef & Prunes Stew .................................................. 128

Seafood & Tomato Stew ........................................... 130

Roasted Whole Chicken ........................................... 131

Lemony Chicken Breasts with Yogurt Sauce ............ 132

Chicken Breasts with Balsamic Fig Sauce ................ 134

Bruschetta Chicken Breasts ...................................... 135

Chicken with Caper Sauce ....................................... 136

Braised Chicken with Artichokes ............................. 138

Chicken & Dried Fruit Casserole ............................. 139

Steak with Yogurt Sauce ........................................... 140

Beef & Olives Bake ................................................... 142

Leg of Lamb with Potatoes ....................................... 143

Veggies & Feta Stuffed Leg of Lamb ........................ 145

Spiced Lamb Chops .................................................. 147

Lamb Chops with Herbed Pistachios ....................... 148

- Lamb Chops with Veggies .......................................... 150
- Pork Chops with Balsamic Peach Glaze ................... 151
- Baked Fish with Tomatoes & Capers ....................... 152
- Salmon with Avocado Cream .................................... 154
- Salmon with Fennel & Couscous .............................. 155
- Grilled Salmon ............................................................ 157
- Cod in Spicy Tomato Sauce ...................................... 158
- Halibut Parcel with Olives & Capers ........................ 160
- Tuna with Olives Sauce .............................................. 161
- Tilapia with Capers .................................................... 162
- Tilapia with Chickpeas & Veggies ............................ 164
- Tilapia in Herb Sauce ................................................ 165
- Almond Crusted Tilapia ............................................ 166
- Seafood Paella ............................................................ 167
- Rice & Veggies Jambalaya ......................................... 168
- Quinoa & Lentil Casserole ........................................ 170

14-Day Meal Plan .......................................................... 172

Healthy Tips for Home Cooking .................................. 176

Essential Principles for Weight Loss ............................. 177

Conclusion ..................................................................... 178

# Introduction of Mediterranean Diet

## Chapter-1: Understanding the Mediterranean Diet

### The History of the Mediterranean Diet

The origin of the Mediterranean diet is involved around the area along the Mediterranean Sea. These areas are also known for the initiators for the origins of the culture of the world. The eating habits of the inhabitants of these areas have developed thousands of years ago. The versatility of dietary habits can be seen in parts of Europe including Spain, Greece, Southern France, Italy, and Portugal. The Mediterranean diet can also be seen being followed in the northern parts of Africa like Tunisia and Morocco. The Mediterranean diet is also being followed by the Middle Eastern countries like Syria and Lebanon as well as by Balkan states and Turkey. The diet is too much popular because the region produces fresh veggies and fruits around the year and is consumed by people frequently. The main produce of the area includes nuts, olive oil, legumes, bread, wine and an abundant supply of fish from the Mediterranean Sea itself. Meal prepping and sharing it with others is a cultural root of the Mediterranean region and the cuisine is popular across the globe for its rich and delicious taste and flavor.

## What is the Mediterranean Diet?

The Mediterranean diet is based upon the cuisines and culture of the Mediterranean region. Numerous scientific and medical studies have argued and proven that the Mediterranean diet is very healthy and is a perfect diet plan for avoiding various chronic diseases like cancer, cardiac complications and also for boosting life expectancy.

Back in the 1950s, the medical researchers had started drawing connections between diet and cardiac complications. Dr. Ancel Keys performed a study on various diets in accordance with the principles of epidemiology. The study is known as "Seven Countries Study" and has been declared the most authentic epidemiological studies ever conducted. The study involved around 13,000 male individuals from the US, Japan, Serbia, Finland, the Netherlands, and Croatia and was performed over a decade. The study was concluded on the fact that the people from the Mediterranean region had a smaller risk of getting a chronic disease related to heart an enjoyed more healthy lifestyles as compared to the rest of the world. The study also argued that the mortality rate of the Mediterranean region was comparatively low from the rest of the globe too i.e. Greek men aged between 50 to 54 had 90% lower risk of having a cardiac issue as compared to the same age group from the US.

The study also showed that the Mediterranean diet is rich in fat content has 40% of its calories subjected to its high fat. The Mediterranean diet is very different in its fat intake from the rest of the diets. Mediterranean cuisine involves higher content of unsaturated fat like olive oil and lower content of saturated fats. Saturated fats are mainly present in dairy products and meat apart from their slight presence in a few nuts, avocados and certain vegetable oils. The saturated fats are utilized by the body to make cholesterol and this has been proven various times that cardiovascular issues are strongly linked with higher cholesterol levels.

There are many scientific types of research that have further backed the work of Dr. Ancle Keys about the healthy lifestyle of the Mediterranean people. An analysis issued by the WHO in 1990 argued that Europe Mediterranean countries like Italy, Greece, France, and Spain have a lower risk of heart complications, higher life expectancy and lower risk of cancer from the rest of Europe. The analysis proved critical as these countries have high smoking populations and aren't having any properly conducted exercise programs like American society. This indicates that this healthy lifestyle has some other factors involved. The factor of genetic variations has also been discarded by scientists because those Mediterranean who move out to other countries and get off from the Mediterranean diet also lose the health advantages the diet offered. These studies all ponder the fact that both lifestyle and diet are critically important factors. In 1994, a French study argued that people following the Mediterranean diet are less prone to have cardiac diseases and deaths as compared to other diet followers.

The Mediterranean diet came into the limelight when the head of the Nutrition Department of Harvard University, Dr. Walter Willet recommended it to various people. Low-fat oriented diets were already being prescribed for heart issues. Mediterranean groups involved in his studies had a high-fat oriented diet which has its main fat content from olive oil. His studies argued that the risk of heart-related complications and diseases can be lowered by increasing the intake of a type of dietary fat i.e. the monosaturated fat, which is present mostly in olive oils. This argument of Dr. Walter was completely opposite to the generally applied nutritional preferences and recommendations of eliminating all kind of fat content from diet plans to avoid heart-related problems. Studies have concluded that unsaturated fats have been credited with a high amount of HDL cholesterol which is also referred to as "the good" cholesterol. The reason for HDL cholesterol being credited as a friend for the body is that protects the body from cardiovascular complications. Dr. Willet also drew the links between meat intake with cancer and cardiovascular diseases.

Dr. Willet and the WHO along with various other researchers joined hands in 1994 and constructed the Mediterranean Food Pyramid. The Mediterranean Food Pyramid involves food from various categories and its intake amount per day to perfectly follow the Mediterranean diet plan. These researchers argue that their food groups are far more beneficial in health status as compared to the food groups designed by the USDA (United States Department of Agriculture). The USDA has listed a higher content of daily meat and dairy servings. The Mediterranean diet specialists claim that these recommendations are politically motivated and have nothing to do with dietary science at all.

## Description of the Mediterranean Diet:

The Mediterranean diet plan has various specific characteristics which make it different from other diet plans.

These include the following:

1. The major portion of the diet plan is derived from various plant related sources like bread, rice, fruits, legumes (lentils and beans), whole grains, pasta, couscous and bulgur (from wheat), potatoes, polenta (from corn), nuts and seeds.
2. The leading source of fat in the diet is olive oil and is used as the main cooking oil too. It is used in abundance and approximately 35% of the calories are because of the fats. The important thing to understand is that saturated fats are only credited with 8% of the total calories only and is even lesser than this in some cases, which means that the consumption of dairy products and meat is limited.
3. Veggies and fruits intake is high in numbers. Both veggies and fruits are unprocessed, locally produced, fresh and eaten in season.
4. Dairy intake is limited in the Mediterranean diet plan. Dairy is consumed mostly in the form of yogurt and cheese with their amounts being 1 cup of yogurt and 1 oz. of cheese.
5. Eggs are consumed around four eggs per week.
6. Poultry and fish are allowed only one to three times a week. This means that it should be lower than 1 lb. per week collectively, and fish should be preferred over poultry.
7. Red meat is also consumed in a limited amount i.e. once in a month while its quantity should be less than a pound in a single month.
8. Honey is the main sweetening source in the Mediterranean diet. Sweet intake is also limited in

this diet plan and is allowed for consumption a few times every week.
9. Wine intake is moderated in nature and is allowed 1-2 glasses every day.

**Benefits of the Mediterranean Diet**

As explained above, the Mediterranean diet has various health benefits for its followers if it's followed consistently. Some of the most important ones are as follows:

1. **Preserve Memory:**

    The Mediterranean diet is proven to be very beneficial in preserving your memory and preventing cognitive declines. The reason is that the Mediterranean diet is high in its healthy fat content which is super beneficial for stimulating the human brain power as well as avoiding or lowering the risk of cognitive decline and dementia. A study claims constantly following the Mediterranean diet will reduce the risk of cognitive declines by around 40 percent.

2. **Lower Risk of Cardiovascular Complications:**

    The Mediterranean diet has a strong positive effect on heart-related risk factors like triglycerides, high BP and cholesterol. This is why it reduces the risk of having cardiovascular diseases like strokes, myocardial infarction (commonly known as a heart attack) and coronary heart disease, etc.

3. **Bone Strengthening:**

    Olive oil is used in abundance in the Mediterranean diet. Olive oil is credited with preserving and increasing bone density by incrementing the maturity and proliferation of the bone cells. The diet patterns of the Mediterranean diet are also credited with avoiding osteoporosis.

4. **Blood Sugar Controlling:**

The Mediterranean diet has been proven to control body blood sugar and diabetes. It is proven by a study that it can also reverse type-2 diabetes. It is also claimed that it can improve heart-related risks and blood sugar control in individuals already having it. The Mediterranean diet followers when observed showed, improved blood sugar, improved weight loss, lower urge to get medical treatment as compared to those having a low-fat diet plan.

5. **Anti-Depression:**

The Mediterranean diet has also been credited as an anti-depressant. A study conducted in 2013 showed that those who follow the Mediterranean diet plan has approximately 98.6% reduced risk of prone to depression than those who follow other diet plans.

6. **Prevents Cancer:**

The Mediterranean diet has been credited with anticancer properties. A study shows that those who follow the Mediterranean diet have a 13% reduced risk of having terminal cancer than those who don't follow the diet. The various cancers which can be prevented by following the Mediterranean diet include neck cancer, liver cancer, breast cancer, prostate cancer, head cancer, colorectal cancer, and gastric cancer.

# Chapter-2: Starting the Mediterranean Diet

**Planning the Mediterranean Diet**

Although you can find numerous cookbook and recipe pamphlets for starting a Mediterranean diet, we are going to explain the basic steps which lead toward the Mediterranean diet. These include:

1. The first step involves eliminating all kinds of oils, margarine, and butter by replacing it with olive oil.
2. Always consume meats with salads and bread.
3. American followers can visit farmer markets or places selling organic produce to grab themselves fresh veggies and fruits.
4. Replace meat by legumes, whole grains and other foods for various meals.
5. Always have cheese or yogurt instead of milk.
6. Various other factors include having workout sessions to wade-off stress.
7. The largest meal i.e. the lunch should be followed with a siesta.

**Precautions:**

1. Don't consume wine if you are having any health complications.
2. Only use olive oil in abundance when it is the sole oil in your food, not as additional oil.
3. Lower fat intake from dairy products, hydrogenated cooking oils, and other sources.

**The Top 10 Tips to Success**

The Mediterranean diet has been credited with a lot of health benefits which can be easily gained by simple tricks. The following tips and tricks are going to ensure you're perfectly following up on the Mediterranean diet. These include:

1. **Doubling or Tripling your Veggies:**

    An increased amount of veggies is always beneficial for your health. There are numerous researches which prove that any plant-heavy diet plan has far better health benefits than any other diet plan. According to a study, people who consume 7 or above servings of veggies and fruits have a comparatively lower risk of cardiovascular diseases and cancer. As per the findings of another study, 10 or above servings of fruits and veggies will reduce the risk of strokes and avoid 7.8 million premature deaths.

2. **Start loving legumes:**

    Legumes are the richest protein resource included in the Mediterranean diet and they are also credited as the perfect dietary fiber resource available. A single cup of navy beans has more dietary fiber than 7 slices of bread (whole-wheat) and more protein than 2 eggs. Eat more of them.

3. **Consume enough Seafood and Fish:**

    Seafood and fishes are high n proteins, vitamin B & D, selenium and are also supported by a study that explains how consumption of 2 oz. of fish can lower the risk of death by 12 %. You should preferably consume fatty fishes.

4. **Start using Olive oil:**

The first step for a successful Mediterranean diet is to eliminate all kinds of oils, margarine, and butter by replacing it with olive oil. There are beneficial mono-saturated fats in olive oil which produce HDL cholesterol. HDL cholesterol is credited with preventing heart issues.

5. **Use fruits as desserts:**

    Fruits are low in fat, high in fiber and also perfect antioxidants. Consuming whole-fruits can lower the risk of diabetes. For example, pears and apples are credited with lowering the risk of having heart strokes. You can use fruits as desserts or even snack them between meals.

6. **Garnish using Diary:**

    Allowed dairy products for the Mediterranean diet can be used in small amounts for garnishing. Dairy has been credited with a lower risk of heart diseases, diabetes, obesity, and metabolic syndrome.

7. **Increase seasonings:**

    The Mediterranean diet is very dependent on herbs and seasonings instead of salt like the American diet. Garlic is having nutrients which lower bad cholesterol, promote healthy immune functioning, lowers risk of cancer. Herbs are also antioxidants in nature and can avoid various diseases.

8. **Limit Meat Consumption:**

    The regular Mediterranean diet doesn't have a high content of meats apart from religious events. Even when meat is used, it is grass-fed and pasture-raised and contains a higher amount of Omega-3 fatty acids and CLA.

9. **Eat Pasta:**
Pasta is made from durum and is less likely to spike-up your blood sugar levels. You can combine pasta and olive oil for slowing down absorption.

10. **Socialize your Eating habits:**
There is no concept of fast food in the Mediterranean diet so you don't have to eat alone, rather prefer eating with your family and loved ones to have a better taste of food and life.

# Chapter-3: Foods to Eat

The Mediterranean diet has vast delicious food options for its followers. The exact foods for the diet seem to be controversial as there is certainly variation between the counties. The foods which are preferred to be consumed for perfectly following the Mediterranean diet include:

1. **Veggies** like, kale, carrots, broccoli, tomatoes, cauliflower, Brussels sprouts, spinach, cucumbers, etc.
2. **Fruits** like oranges, strawberries, figs, peaches, melons, pears, apples, dates, bananas, grapes, etc.
3. **Seeds and nuts** like macadamia nuts, cashews, pumpkin seeds, almonds, walnuts, hazelnuts, sunflower seeds, etc.
4. **Legumes** like lentils, chickpeas, beans, pulses, peas, peanuts, etc.

5. **Tubers** like yams, sweet potatoes, turnips, potatoes, etc.
6. **Poultry** like turkey, chicken, duck, etc.
7. **Dairy products** like Greek yogurt, cheese, yogurt, etc.
8. **Eggs** like quail eggs, duck eggs, and chicken eggs, etc.
9. **Spices and Herbs** like basil, rosemary, nutmeg, pepper, mint, garlic, sage, cinnamon, etc.
10. **Healthy fats** like avocado oil, olive oil, olives, and avocados, etc.
11. **Whole grains** like rye, corn, barley, wheat oats, whole wheat, pasta and braid (whole grain), corn, brown rice, etc.
12. **Seafood and Fish** like tuna, trout, shrimp, clams, trout, crabs, sardines, mussels, salmon, etc.

**Beverages:**

- The preferred beverage for the Mediterranean diet is water.
- Apart from this, you can have approximately 1-2 glasses of wine too daily. But you should wine if you have any complications related to its intake.
- You can also drink tea and coffee, but it's preferable to avoid high-sugar drinks, sugar-sweetened beverages, and various fruit juices.

The important factors regarding food that should be kept in mind while following the Mediterranean diet are:

- ➤ Rarely eat red meat.
- ➤ Moderately eat dairy products and poultry.
- ➤ You can eat the rest of the foods in abundance.

*Thanks again for choosing this book,* make sure to leave a short review on Amazon if you enjoy it, I'd love to know what you think. **Thank you!!**

# Chapter-4: Foods to Avoid

As stated earlier, the Mediterranean diet has vast delicious food options for its followers but there is are certain limitations to it too. The foods which are preferred to be avoided for perfectly following the Mediterranean diet include:

1. **Added sugars** like soda, ice cream, soda, table sugar, and various other same products, etc.
2. **Trans Fats** containing foods like margarine and other processed foods.
3. **Refined oils** like cottonseed oil, canola oil, soybean oil, etc.
4. **Processed meats** like hot dogs, processed sausages, etc.
5. **Highly processed foods** i.e. anything labeled "low-fat" or "diet", which indicates that they have been manufactured in a factory.

# Chapter 5: What is the Mediterranean Diet Pyramid?

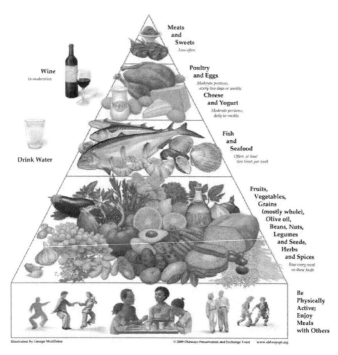

The Mediterranean Diet pyramid is basically a nutritional tool book and was produced by the joint venture of the World Health Organization, the Harvard School of Public Health, and the Oldways Preservation Trust in the year 1993. This guide is based on how you should eat on the Mediterranean Diet, what type and how much you should eat on a daily basis.

The Mediterranean Diet Pyramid is developed on the basis of present-day studies on nutrition and the eating habits of the areas of Italy, Greece, and Crete in the 1960s. it was the time in which life expectancy was all-time high and chronic diseases were very rare irrespective of limited medical facilities. The Pyramid offers a frequency range from days, weeks, to months but fails to deliver the portion sizes.

According to various researches, the Pyramid is committed to promoting healthy and longer lifespan. The Mediterranean Diet Pyramid also lowers down the risk of various chronic diseases like Alzheimer's disease, lung diseases, asthma, etc.

## How to utilize the Mediterranean Diet Plan for effective weight loss?

There is a potential risk of gaining weight because of excessive calorie intake as the portion sizes on the Mediterranean Diet Pyramid aren't mentioned. You can opt for the Harvard Healthy Eating Plans along the Mediterranean Diet Pyramid to make your diet plan more effective in maintaining a proper weight loss. The Harvard Healthy Eating Plans gives a better insight into proportions per meal and can ease your weight loss effectively.

The olive oil and lower processed food intake supports the

weight loss cause and if you carry the diet plan throughout, without any issues, your weight loss is going to be steady and effective. The proper limitation of calorie intake is also the key to maintaining a steady weight loss approach.

Weight loss is always a tricky business for people across the globe when it comes to choosing your diet plan specifically to target your weight. The Mediterranean diet is a good ix but it doesn't get you your desired results immediately. You have to work hard and be consistent to follow the plan to have a strategic weight loss for a longer time. For having a perfect weight loss goal, you have to focus on the changes in lifestyle, command your calorie content by equating your food choices and their portions, and of course workout properly on a regular basis.

### 1. Focusing on changes in lifestyle:

The Mediterranean diet is always about drafting your lifestyle according to the diet plan. The problem with other weight loss plans is that they aren't a fix for a longer time, so you have to manage your portion sizes and calorie intake while on the Mediterranean diet plan to achieve a weight loss for a longer time span. Managing your workout sessions and food can play a critical role in not only a successful weight loss bit also generating healthy habits. For a better change in your lifestyle follow:

- Go for achievable, measurable, and more real aims.

- Restrict diets immediately.

- Manage your time properly for your workouts.
- Go for manageable goals set at a smaller level steadily.

## 2. The Calorie Thing:

Calories play a critical role in your weight loss. Calories define the total energy you consume from foods and the energy which your body utilizes for its working. Calorie burning is very different in people depending on their metabolism rate. Calorie burning is also based on your physical fitness, age, gender, and genetically make. Weight loss is not achieved by eating more calories than your body burns. You have to make a calorie deficit by measuring the number of calories your body burns. Go for a reduction in portion sizes and working out regularly to manage your calorie intake.

## 3. More food yet Weight Reduction:

The Mediterranean diet plan offers a lot of food in your plate on the expense of a few calories and that makes it the best of all. Go for less high-calorie meats and grain and focus more on low-calorie veggies. In addition to this, these foods make you feel more satisfied and make you feel full.

## 4. Adjust your Portion Sizes:

Measuring your portion sizing is more effective than counting calories while planning to decrease their intake. There is a major difference between portion sizes in the USA and the Mediterranean region which is why the people of the latter region are more successful in managing their weights.

### 5. Check for Fat Calories:

The allowed fat content in the Mediterranean diet plan is a bit above the limit in the US, i.e. 35 percent in the Mediterranean region while 30 percent in the USA calories are credited to fat content. The Mediterranean diet lets you count your calories from fat too. The fat content in this region is mostly healthy like from olive oil.

### 6. Boost your Work Out Sessions:

Work out and exercising plays a pivotal role in managing your calories. You have to perform physical activates so that you can burn the leftover calories in your body so that they don't add to your weight. Exercise not only burns your calories but also manages a healthy heart, stress, and increments your energy levels of tour body.

### 7. Curb your hunger:

The Mediterranean diet plan is very effective in suppressing your hunger which is very important and useful in weight reduction. The combo of the accurate plant-based foods and of course healthy fats, your body naturally tends to set its metabolism and makes you feel full for a longer time span.

- Eat more fiber-based foods.

- Stimulate your fullness hormones by following the plan strictly. The Mediterranean diet plan is having an abundant amount of low-glycemic and has foods which illicit any spikes in the blood sugar.

  You can control your appetite by controlling these hormones and your weight reduction will be evident soon.

- Avoid any spikes in blood sugar.

- Have a little amount of fat and go for foods rich in protein content.

# Breakfast Recipes

## Date & Yogurt Smoothie

**Yield:** 2 servings
**Preparation Time:** 10 minutes

**Ingredients:**

- 4 Medjool date, pitted and chopped roughly
- 1 cup plain Greek yogurt
- 2 tablespoons almond butter
- 1 cup fresh apple juice
- 1 cup of ice cubes, crushed

**Instructions:**

1. In a high-speed blender, add all the ingredients and pulse until smooth and creamy.
2. Transfer the smoothie into 2 serving glasses and serve immediately.

### **Blueberry & Banana Smoothie**

**Yield:** 2 servings
**Preparation Time:** 10 minutes

**Ingredients:**

- 2 cups fresh blueberries
- 1 large banana, peeled and cut into chunks
- 2 cups almond milk
- ½ cup of ice cubes, crushed

**Instructions:**

1. In a high-speed blender, add all the ingredients and pulse until smooth and creamy.
2. Transfer the smoothie into 2 serving glasses and serve immediately.

**Mixed Fruit Smoothie**
**Yield:** 2 servings
**Preparation Time:** 10 minutes

**Ingredients:**

- 1 banana, peeled and cut into chunks
- ¾ cup frozen mango chunks
- ¾ cup of frozen strawberries
- 1 tablespoon honey
- ¼ teaspoon ground turmeric
- ¼ teaspoon ground ginger
- ½ cup plain Greek yogurt
- 1 cup of soy milk

**Instructions:**

1. In a high-speed blender, add all the ingredients and pulse until smooth and creamy.
2. Transfer the smoothie into 2 serving glasses and serve immediately.

## Green Fruity Smoothie

**Yield:** 2 servings
**Preparation Time:** 10 minutes

**Ingredients:**

- 2 cups fresh spinach
- 1 small avocado, peeled, pitted and chopped roughly
- 1 large frozen banana, peeled and cut into chunks
- ½ cup frozen pineapple chunks
- 1 scoop protein powder
- 2 tablespoons raw hemp seeds
- 2 teaspoons maca powder
- 1½ cups unsweetened almond milk

**Instructions:**

1. In a high-speed blender, add all the ingredients and pulse until smooth and creamy.
2. Transfer the smoothie into 2 serving glasses and serve immediately.

### Strawberry Smoothie Bowl

**Yield:** 2 servings
**Preparation Time:** 10 minutes

**Ingredients:**

**For Smoothie Bowl:**

- 2 cups frozen strawberries
- 1 banana, peeled and cut into chunks
- 1/3 cup Whey Protein Powder
- 2 tablespoons organic acai powder
- 2 cups almond milk

**For Topping:**

- 2 tablespoons granola
- 1 teaspoon chia seeds
- 1 small banana, peeled and sliced

**Instructions:**

1. For smoothie bowl: in a high-speed blender, add all the ingredients and pulse until well combined.
2. Transfer the mixture into 2 serving bowls evenly.
3. Top each bowl with the granola, chia seed, and banana slices and serve immediately.

## Yogurt Bowl with Caramelized Figs

**Yield:** 4 servings
**Preparation Time:** 10 minutes
**Cooking Time:** 7 minutes

### Ingredients:

- 3 tablespoons honey, divided
- 8 ounces fresh figs, halved
- 2 cups plain Greek yogurt
- ¼ cup pistachios, chopped
- Pinch of ground cinnamon

### Instructions:

1. In a medium skillet, add 1 tablespoon of the honey over medium heat and cook for about 1-2 minutes or until heated.
2. In the skillet, place the figs, cut sides down and cook for about 5 minutes or until caramelized.
3. Remove from the heat and set aside for about 2-3 minutes.
4. Divide the yogurt into serving bowls and top each with the caramelized fig halves.
5. Sprinkle with the pistachios and cinnamon.
6. Drizzle each bowl with the remaining honey and serve.

## Yogurt & Pomegranate Bowl

**Yield:** 2 servings
**Preparation Time:** 10 minutes

### Ingredients:

- 2 cups plain Greek yogurt
- ¾ cup fresh pomegranate seeds
- 2 teaspoons honey

### Instructions:

1. Divide the yogurt into 2 serving bowls evenly and top with pomegranate seeds
2. Drizzle with honey and serve.


## Avocado Toast

**Yield:** 4 servings
**Preparation Time:** 15 minutes
**Cooking Time:** 16 minutes

### Ingredients:

- 1 large avocado, peeled, pitted and chopped roughly
- ¼ teaspoon fresh lemon juice
- 2 tablespoons fresh mint leaves, chopped finely
- Salt and freshly ground black pepper, to taste
- 4 large rye bread slices
- 2 tablespoons feta cheese, crumbled

**Instructions:**

1. In a bowl, add the avocado flesh and with a fork, mash roughly.
2. Add the lemon juice, mint, salt, and black pepper and stir to combine well.
3. Heat a nonstick frying pan over medium-high heat and toast 1 bread slice for about 2 minutes.
4. Carefully, flip the side and toast for about 2 minutes.
5. Repeat with the remaining slices.
6. Arrange the bread slices onto serving plates.
7. Place the avocado mixture over each bread slice and spread in an even layer.
8. Sprinkle each slice with the feta cheese and serve immediately.

**Smoked Salmon Toast**

**Yield:** 2 servings
**Preparation Time:** 15 minutes
**Cooking Time:** 6 minutes

**Ingredients:**

- 1 teaspoon white vinegar
- 2 eggs, at room temperature
- 2 bread slices, toasted
- 2 ounces avocado, peeled, pitted and chopped roughly
- ¼ teaspoon fresh lemon juice
- Salt, to taste
- 3½ ounces smoked salmon

- Dash of soy sauce
- Freshly cracked black pepper, to taste
- 1 tablespoon scallions, sliced thinly

**Instructions:**

1. Fill a small pan with water about one-third full and bring to a boil over high heat.
2. Stir in the vinegar and reduce the heat to medium-low.
3. In a small bowl, crack 1 egg and gently, slide into the simmering water.
4. Lightly poach for about 2-3 minutes.
5. With a slotted spoon, transfer the egg into a bowl of chilled water for about 10 seconds to stop the cooking.
6. Now, transfer the egg onto a paper towel-lined plate to drain.
7. Repeat with the remaining egg.
8. Meanwhile, in a bowl, add the avocado flesh and with a fork, mash roughly.
9. Add the lemon juice and a pinch of salt and mix until well combined.
10. Arrange the bread slices onto serving plates.
11. Place the avocado mixture over each bread slice and spread in an even layer.
12. Top each slice with smoked salmon, followed by 1 poached egg
13. Drizzle each slice with soy sauce and sprinkle with black pepper.
14. Garnish with scallions and serve immediately.

## Tahini & Feta Toast

**Yield:** 2 servings
**Preparation Time:** 15 minutes

**Ingredients:**

- 1½ tablespoons tahini
- 1 tablespoon fresh lemon juice
- 1 teaspoon water
- 2 whole wheat bread slices, toasted
- 2 teaspoons feta cheese, crumbled
- 2 teaspoons pine nuts
- Ground black pepper, to taste

**Instructions:**

1. In a small bowl, add the tahini, lemon juice, and water and mix until a thick mixture is formed.
2. Arrange the bread slices onto serving plates.
3. Place the tahini mixture over each bread slice and spread in an even layer.
4. Top each slice with the feta cheese and pine nuts.
5. Sprinkle with the black pepper and serve immediately.


## Honeyed Ricotta & Peach Toast

**Yield:** 6 servings
**Preparation Time:** 15 minutes
**Cooking Time:** 6 minutes

**Ingredients:**

**For Ricotta Spread**

- 1 cup part-skim whole milk ricotta cheese
- ½ cup almonds, sliced
- 2 teaspoons fresh orange zest, grated
- 1 teaspoon honey
- ¼ teaspoon almond extract

**For Serving**

- 6 whole-grain bread slices, toasted
- 1 peach, halved, pitted and sliced
- 2 teaspoons almonds, sliced
- 3 teaspoons honey

**Instructions:**

1. For ricotta spread: in a medium bowl, add the ricotta cheese, almonds, orange zest, honey, and almond extract and gently stir to combine.
2. Arrange the bread slices onto serving plates.
3. Place the ricotta mixture over each bread slice and spread in an even layer.
4. Top each slice with peach slices, followed by the almond slices.
5. Drizzle with the honey and serve immediately.

## Breakfast Sandwich

**Yield:** 4 servings
**Preparation Time:** 15 minutes
**Cooking Time:** 5 minutes

### Ingredients:

- 4 multigrain sandwich thins
- 4 teaspoons olive oil, divided
- 1 tablespoon fresh rosemary, minced
- 4 eggs
- 2 cups fresh baby spinach leaves
- 1 medium tomato, cut into 8 thin slices
- 4 tablespoons low-fat feta cheese, crumbled
- Salt and freshly ground black pepper, to taste

### Instructions:

1. Preheat the oven to 375 degrees F.
2. Carefully, split each sandwich thin.
3. Brush the cut side of each sandwich thin with 2 teaspoons of the olive oil evenly.
4. Arrange the sandwich thins onto a baking sheet.
5. Bake for about 5 minutes or until edges are lightly brown and crisp.
6. Meanwhile, in a large skillet add the remaining olive oil and rosemary over medium-high heat and cook until heated through.
7. Break eggs, one at a time, into skillet and cook for about 1 minute or until the desired doneness of the eggs.
8. With a spatula, break the yolk of each egg.
9. Carefully, flip the eggs and cook for about 1 minute or until done.

10. Remove from the heat and transfer the eggs onto a large plate.
11. Remove the baking sheet of sandwich thins from the oven.
12. Arrange the bottom halves of the toasted sandwich thins onto 4 serving plates.
13. Top each sandwich thin with spinach, followed by 2 tomato slices, an egg and 1 tablespoon of the feta cheese.
14. Sprinkle each sandwich with the salt and black pepper.
15. Top each with the remaining sandwich thin halves and serve.

## Couscous with Dried Fruit

**Yield:** 4 servings
**Preparation Time:** 15 minutes
**Cooking Time:** 3 minutes

**Ingredients:**

- 3 cups low-fat milk
- 1 cup uncooked whole-wheat couscous
- ¼ cup dried currants
- 1/3 cup dried apricots, chopped
- 6 teaspoons dark brown sugar, divided
- ¼ teaspoon ground cinnamon
- Salt, to taste
- 2 teaspoons unsalted butter, melted

**Instructions:**

1. In a pan, add the milk over medium-high heat and cook for about 3 minutes or until heated through.
2. Remove from the heat and immediately, stir in the couscous, dried fruit, 4 teaspoons of brown sugar, cinnamon and salt.
3. Cover the pan and set aside for about 15 minutes.
4. In 4 serving bowls, divide the couscous mixture.
5. Top with melted butter and remaining brown sugar evenly.
6. Serve immediately.

## Barley with Warm Berry Compote

**Yield:** 4 servings
**Preparation Time:** 15 minutes
**Cooking Time:** 30 minutes

**Ingredients:**

- 3 cups of water
- 1 cup pearl barley
- Kosher salt, to taste
- 2 cups mixed fresh berries (raspberries, blueberries, and blackberries)
- 1½ tablespoons fresh orange juice
- 2 teaspoons chia seeds
- 2 teaspoons fresh orange zest, grated
- 1 teaspoon honey
- 1 cup warm almond milk
- ¼ cup slivered almonds, toasted

**Instructions:**

1. In a pan, add the water, barley and a pinch of salt over medium-high heat and bring to a boil.
2. Reduce the heat to low and simmer, covered for about 25-30 minutes or until all the liquid is absorbed, stirring occasionally.
3. Meanwhile, for berry compote: in another small pan, add the berries, orange juice, chia seeds, orange zest, and honey over medium heat and cook for about 10 minutes, stirring occasionally.
4. Remove from the heat and set aside to cool slightly.
5. In 4 serving bowls, divide the barley evenly.
6. Top each with almond milk, followed by the berry compote and almonds evenly.
7. Serve immediately.

**Spiced Quinoa Porridge**

**Yield:** 4 servings
**Preparation Time:** 10 minutes
**Cooking Time:** 15 minutes

**Ingredients:**

- 1 cup uncooked red quinoa, rinsed and drained
- 2 cups of water
- ½ teaspoon vanilla extract
- ½ cup of coconut milk
- ¼ teaspoon fresh lemon peel, grated finely

- 10-12 drops liquid stevia
- 1 teaspoon ground cinnamon
- ½ teaspoons ground ginger
- ½ teaspoon ground nutmeg
- Pinch of ground cloves
- 1 cup fresh strawberries, hulled and sliced

**Instructions:**

1. In a large pan, mix together the quinoa, water and vanilla extract over medium heat and bring to a boil.
2. Reduce the heat to low and simmer, covered for about 15 minutes or until all the liquid is absorbed, stirring occasionally.
3. In the pan of the quinoa, add the coconut milk, lemon peel, stevia, and spices and stir to combine.
4. Immediately, remove from the heat and with a fork, fluff the quinoa.
5. Divide the quinoa mixture into serving bowls evenly
6. Serve with the topping of strawberry slices.

### Fruity Quinoa Bowl

**Yield:** 2 servings
**Preparation Time:** 15 minutes
**Cooking Time:** 15 minutes

### Ingredients:

- ½ cup uncooked quinoa, rinsed and drained
- ½ cup skim milk
- ½ cup of water
- ½ teaspoon vanilla extract
- ½ teaspoon ground cinnamon
- ½ cup dried cherries
- ½ cup cashews, chopped
- 1 tablespoon honey
- ½ cup fresh blackberries

### Instructions:

1. In a pan, add the quinoa, milk, water, vanilla extract and cinnamon over medium heat and bring to a boil.
2. Reduce the heat to medium-low and simmer, covered for about 10-15 minutes or until all the liquid is absorbed, stirring occasionally.
3. Remove from the heat and stir in the cherries, cashews, and honey.
4. Divide the quinoa mixture into serving bowls evenly
5. Serve with the topping of blackberries.

## Overnight Quinoa with Dried Fruit

**Yield:** 4 servings
**Preparation Time:** 10 minutes
**Cooking Time:** 15 minutes

**Ingredients:**

- 1 cup uncooked red quinoa, rinsed and drained
- 2 cups of water
- 8 dried apricot halves, chopped into-sized pieces
- 8 smaller dried figs, chopped into-sized pieces
- ¼ cup walnuts, chopped into-sized pieces
- 1 teaspoon ground cinnamon
- 2 cups almond milk

**Instructions:**

1. In a large pan, add the quinoa and water over medium heat and bring to a boil.
2. Reduce the heat to low and simmer, covered for about 15 minutes or until all the liquid is absorbed, stirring occasionally.
3. Meanwhile, in a large bowl, add the apricots, figs, walnuts, and cinnamon and mix well.
4. Remove the pan of quinoa from the heat and with a fork, fluff it.
5. Add the quinoa into the bowl of dried fruit mixture and toss to coat well.
6. Divide the quinoa mixture into 4 mason jars and top each with a ½ cup of the almond milk.
7. Cover the jars and refrigerate overnight before serving.

## Spiced Quinoa & Banana Bake

**Yield:** 6 servings
**Preparation Time:** 15 minutes
**Cooking Time:** 1 hour 19 minutes

**Ingredients:**

- 3 cups ripe bananas, peeled and mashed
- ¼ cup pure maple syrup
- ¼ cup molasses
- 2 teaspoons vanilla extract
- 1 tablespoon ground cinnamon
- 1 teaspoon ground cloves
- 1 teaspoon ground ginger
- ½ teaspoon ground allspice
- ½ teaspoon salt
- 1 cup uncooked red quinoa, rinsed and drained
- 2½ cups unsweetened vanilla almond milk
- ¼ cup slivered almonds

**Instructions:**

1. In the bottom of a 2½-3-quart casserole dish, add the mashed bananas, maple syrup, molasses, vanilla extract, spices, and salt, and mix until well combined.
2. Add the quinoa and stir to combine well.
3. Add the almond milk and mix until well combined.
4. Cover the casserole dish and refrigerate overnight.
5. Preheat the oven to 350 degrees F.
6. Remove the casserole dish from the refrigerator with a fork, beat the quinoa mixture well.

7. With a piece of foil, cover the casserole dish and bake for about 1-1¼ hours or until all the liquid is absorbed and the top of the quinoa is set.
8. Now, set the oven to broiler on high.
9. Remove the foil and sprinkle the top of quinoa mixture with sliced almonds.
10. With a spatula, press the almonds into the quinoa mixture lightly.
11. Broil for about 2-4 minutes.
12. Remove from the oven and set aside to cool for about 10 minutes.
13. Cut the casserole into desired sized pieces and serve.


**Overnight Fruity Oatmeal**

**Yield:** 10 servings
**Preparation Time:** 15 minutes

**Ingredients:**

- 10 ounces fresh strawberries
- 2 ripe bananas, peeled and cut into chunks
- 3 cups gluten-free rolled oats
- ½ cup unsweetened coconut, shredded
- ½ cup walnuts, chopped
- 1/3 cup chia seeds
- 2 tablespoons agave syrup
- 4 cups almond milk
- 2-3 cups mixed fresh berries

**Instructions:**

1. In a high-speed blender, add the strawberries and bananas and pulse until pureed.
2. In a large mixing bowl, add the oats, coconut, walnuts and chia seeds and mix well.
3. Add the pureed fruit mixture, agave syrup, and almond milk and mix until well combined.
4. Cover the bowl and refrigerate overnight.
5. Divide the oatmeal into serving bowls evenly.
6. Serve with the topping of berries.

## Overnight Oatmeal with Figs

**Yield:** 2 servings
**Preparation Time:** 10 minutes

**Ingredients:**

- ½ cup quick oats
- 2 tablespoons almonds, chopped
- 1 tablespoon chia seeds
- 1 cup unsweetened soy milk
- 1 tablespoon honey
- 2-3 fresh figs, sliced

**Instructions:**

1. In a large bowl, add the oats, almonds, chia seeds, and soy milk and mix until well combined.
2. Cover the bowl and refrigerate overnight.
3. Serve with the topping of berries
4. Cover the bowl and refrigerate overnight.

Mediterranean Diet For Beginners

5. Divide the oatmeal into serving bowls evenly and drizzle with the honey.
6. Serve with the topping of fig slices.

### Oatmeal & Yogurt Bowl

**Yield:** 2 servings
**Preparation Time:** 15 minutes
**Cooking Time:** 1 hour 19 minutes

**Ingredients:**

- 2 cups of water
- 1 cup old fashioned oats
- 2 tablespoons tahini
- 1 tablespoon honey
- 1 tablespoon fresh lemon juice
- ¼ teaspoon ground allspice
- 1 (7-ounce) container plain Greek yogurt
- ¼ teaspoon ground cinnamon
- 2 tablespoons fresh blueberries
- 2 tablespoons pistachios, chopped
- 

**Instructions:**

1. In a pan, add the water over medium heat and bring to a boil.
2. Stir in the oats and cook about 5 minutes, stirring occasionally.
3. Meanwhile, for the sauce: in a small blender, add the tahini, honey, lemon juice, and allspice and pulse until smooth.

4. Remove the pan of oats from the heat and stir in the half of the yogurt and cinnamon.
5. Divide the oatmeal into serving bowls evenly.
6. Top each bowl with the remaining yogurt, followed by the blueberries and pistachios.
7. Drizzle with the tahini sauce and serve.

## Strawberry & Yogurt Muffins

**Yield:** 9 servings
**Preparation Time:** 20 minutes
**Cooking Time:** 20 minutes

### Ingredients:

- 1½ cups fresh strawberries, hulled and chopped roughly
- 1-2 teaspoons balsamic vinegar
- 2 teaspoons white sugar
- Pinch of freshly ground black pepper
- 1½ cups whole-wheat flour
- 1½ cup all-purpose flour
- 1 tablespoon baking powder
- ½ teaspoon baking soda
- ½ teaspoon salt
- ½ cup brown sugar
- 7½ tablespoons olive oil
- 2 eggs
- 1½ cups low-fat Greek yogurt
- 2 teaspoons vanilla extract
- ½ teaspoon almond extract

**Instructions:**

1. Ina glass bowl, add the strawberries, vinegar, white sugar, and black pepper and mix well.
2. Cover the bowl and set aside for an hour.
3. Preheat the oven to 400 degrees F. Line 18 cups of 2 muffin tins with paper liners.
4. In a large bowl, add the flours, baking powder, baking soda, and salt and with a wire whisk, mix well.
5. In another large bowl, add the brown sugar and olive oil and mix until well combined and smooth.
6. Add the eggs, one at a time, mixing well after each addition.
7. And the yogurt, vanilla extract and almond extract and mix until well combined.
8. Add the flour mixture and mix until just combined.
9. Gently, fold in the strawberries.
10. Transfer the mixture into the prepared muffin cups evenly.
11. Bake for about 18-20 minutes or until a toothpick inserted in the center comes out clean.
12. Remove from the oven and place onto the wire racks to cool in the pans for about 5 minutes.
13. Carefully, invert the muffins onto the wire racks to cool completely before serving.

## Nutty & Fruity Oat Muffins

**Yield:** 6 servings
**Preparation Time:** 20 minutes
**Cooking Time:** 22 minutes

### Ingredients:

- Olive oil cooking spray
- 1 cup whole-wheat pastry flour
- 1 cup oats
- 1/3 cup sugar
- 1 teaspoon baking powder
- ½ teaspoon baking soda
- ½ teaspoon salt
- 1 egg, beaten lightly
- ¾ cup natural applesauce
- 1 cup low-fat buttermilk
- 1¼ teaspoons vanilla extract
- 1 cup fresh blueberries
- ¼ cup dates, pitted and chopped
- 2 teaspoons fresh orange zest, grated finely
- ¾ cup walnuts, toasted and chopped roughly
- ¼ cup boiling water

### Instructions:

1. Preheat the oven to 375 degrees F. Grease a 12 cups muffin tin with the cooking spray.
2. In a mixing bowl, add the flour, oats, baking powder, baking soda, and salt and with a wire whisk, mix well.

3. In another large bowl, add the egg, applesauce, buttermilk, and vanilla extract and beat until well combined.
4. Add the flour mixture and mix until just combined.
5. Gently, fold in the blueberries, dates, orange zest and walnuts.
6. Add the water and gently, stir to combine.
7. Set the mixture aside for about 10-15 minutes.
8. Now, transfer the mixture into the prepared muffin cups evenly.
9. Bake for about 20-22 minutes or until a toothpick inserted in the center comes out clean.
10. Remove from the oven and place onto a wire rack to cool in the pan for about 5 minutes.
11. Carefully, invert the muffins onto the wire rack to cool completely before serving.

## Quinoa & Veggie Muffins

**Yield:** 6 servings
**Preparation Time:** 20 minutes
**Cooking Time:** 35 minutes

### Ingredients:

- Olive oil cooking spray
- 2 teaspoons sunflower oil
- ½ cup onion, chopped finely
- 1 cup cherry tomatoes, sliced
- 2 cups fresh baby spinach, chopped finely
- ½ cup Kalamata olives, pitted and chopped
- 1 tablespoon fresh oregano, chopped
- 8 eggs
- 1 cup cooked quinoa
- 1 cup feta cheese, crumbled
- Salt, to taste

### Instructions:

1. Preheat the oven to 350 degrees F. Grease a 12 cups muffin tin with the cooking spray.
2. In a skillet, heat the oil over medium heat and sauté the onion for about 2-3 minutes.
3. Add the tomatoes and sauté for about 1 minute.
4. Add the spinach and sauté for about 1 minute.
5. Remove from the heat and stir in the olives and oregano.
6. In a bowl, crack the eggs and beat slightly.
7. Add the quinoa, feta cheese, veggie mixture, and salt and mix until well combined.
8. Divide the mixture into prepared muffin cups evenly.

9. Bake for about 30 minutes or until tops become light golden brown.
10. Remove from the oven and place the muffin tin onto a wire rack to cool for about 5 minutes.
11. Carefully, invert the muffins onto a platter and serve warm.

**Cheesy Veggie Muffins**

**Yield:** 6 servings
**Preparation Time:** 20 minutes
**Cooking Time:** 12 minutes

**Ingredients:**

- Olive oil cooking spray
- ¼ cup half-and-half
- 6 large eggs
- Salt and freshly ground black pepper, to taste
- ½ cup sun-dried tomatoes in oil, drained and chopped
- 1/3 cup canned Kalamata olives, drained, pitted and quartered
- ¼ cup bottled sweet red peppers, drained and chopped
- ¼ cup canned artichokes in oil drained and sliced thinly
- ¼ cup Asiago cheese, shredded
- ¼ cup feta cheese, crumbled
- ¼ cup fresh parsley, chopped

## Instructions:

1. Preheat the oven to 375F. Grease 24 cups of mini muffin tins with the cooking spray.
2. In a bowl, add the half-and-half, eggs, salt, and black pepper and beat until well combined.
3. In another large bowl, add the vegetables and Asiago cheese and mix well.
4. Place the egg mixture into the prepared muffin cups about ¾ of full.
5. Place the vegetable mixture over egg mixture evenly and top with the remaining egg mixture.
6. Sprinkle each cup with feta and parsley evenly.
7. Bake for about 12 minutes or until eggs are done completely.
8. Remove from the oven and place the muffin tin onto a wire rack to cool for about 5 minutes.
9. Carefully, invert the muffins onto a platter and serve warm.

## Baked Yogurt Crepes

**Yield:** 8 servings
**Preparation Time:** 15 minutes
**Cooking Time:** 20 minutes

### Ingredients:

- Olive oil cooking spray
- 2 cups flour
- 1/3 cup sugar plus extra for dusting
- 1 teaspoon baking powder
- ¼ teaspoon baking soda

- Salt, to taste
- 4 ounces of frozen butter
- ½ cup plain Greek yogurt
- 1 large egg

**Instructions:**

1. Preheat the oven to 400 degrees F. Lightly, grease a baking sheet with the cooking spray.
2. In a bowl, add the flour, sugar, baking powder, baking soda, and salt and with a wire whisk, mix well.
3. Reserve some flour mixture in another bowl.
4. Grate the butter in the remaining flour mixture and stir to combine.
5. Add the yogurt and egg and mix until well combined and a chunky dough forms.
6. Place the dough onto a floured surface and with your hands, knead until a sticky dough forms.
7. With a rolling pin, roll the dough into an 8-inch circle.
8. Dust with the reserved flour mixture and with your hands press down the slightly.
9. Sprinkle with the extra sugar.
10. Cut into equal sized 8 wedges and arrange onto the prepared baking sheet in a single layer
11. Bake for about 15 minutes.
12. Remove from the oven and set aside to cool slightly before serving.
13. Serve warm.

## Eggs in Tomato Cups

**Yield:** 4 servings
**Preparation Time:** 15 minutes
**Cooking Time:** 17 minutes

### Ingredients:

- 2 tablespoons olive oil
- 8 medium tomatoes
- 8 large eggs
- ¼ cup unsweetened almond milk
- ¼ cup Parmesan cheese, grated
- Salt and freshly ground black pepper, to taste
- 2 tablespoons mixed fresh herbs (parsley, thyme, rosemary), chopped

### Instructions:

1. Preheat the oven to 375 degrees F. Grease a large, ovenproof skillet with the olive oil.
2. With a small paring knife, cut around the stems of the tomatoes and then, discard them.
3. With a small spoon, carefully scoop out all the seeds and pulp of the tomatoes.
4. Arrange the tomato cups into the prepared skillet, cut side up in a single layer.
5. Carefully, crack an egg into each tomato cup.
6. Top each egg with 1 tablespoon of the almond milk, followed by and 1 tablespoon of the Parmesan cheese.
7. Season each egg with the salt and black pepper.
8. Bake for about 15-17 minutes or until the tomatoes are tender and the egg whites are set.

9. Remove from the oven and set aside for about 5 minutes before serving.
10. Serve immediately with the garnishing of fresh herbs.

## Oat Pancakes

**Yield:** 6 servings
**Preparation Time:** 15 minutes
**Cooking Time:** 24 minutes

**Ingredients:**

- ½ cup all-purpose flour
- 1 cup old-fashioned oats
- 2 tablespoons flax seeds
- 1 teaspoon baking soda
- Salt, as required
- 2 tablespoons agave syrup
- 2 large eggs
- 2 cups low-fat plain Greek yogurt
- 2 tablespoons extra-virgin olive oil

**Instructions:**

1. In a blender, add the flour, oats, flax seeds, baking soda, and salt and pulse until well combined.
2. Transfer the mixture into a large bowl.
3. Add the remaining ingredients except the oil and mix until well combined.
4. Set aside for about 20 minutes before cooking.

5. Heat a large nonstick skillet over medium heat and grease with a little oil.
6. Add a ¼ cup of the mixture and cook for about 2 minutes or until the bottom becomes golden brown.
7. Carefully, flip the side and cook for about 2 minutes more.
8. Repeat with the remaining mixture.
9. Serve warm.

**Eggs in Spicy Veggie Sauce**

**Yield:** 6 servings
**Preparation Time:** 20 minutes
**Cooking Time:** 31 minutes

**Ingredients:**

- 2 tablespoons extra-virgin olive oil
- 1 red bell pepper, seeded and chopped
- 2 small yellow onions, chopped
- 3 garlic cloves, chopped roughly
- 30 ounces tomatoes, chopped finely
- 1 teaspoon sugar
- 1 teaspoon ground coriander
- 1 teaspoon ground cumin
- ¾ teaspoon smoked paprika
- ¼ teaspoon red pepper flakes, crushed
- 1½ teaspoons salt, divided
- 2 cups fresh mixed greens (Swiss chard, kale, spinach), tough ribs removed and chopped finely
- 3 ounces feta cheese, crumbled
- 6 eggs

- ¼ cup fresh cilantro, chopped

**Instructions:**

1. In a large ovenproof skillet, heat the oil over medium heat and cook the bell pepper, onions, and garlic for about 8 minutes, stirring frequently.
2. Stir in the tomatoes, sugar, spices and 1¼ teaspoons of the salt and cook for about 10 minutes, stirring occasionally.
3. Stir in the greens and cook for about 5 minutes, stirring occasionally.
4. Meanwhile, preheat the broiler of oven. Arrange a rack in the top position of the oven.
5. Remove the skillet from the heat and with a spoon, make 6 wells in the greens mixture.
6. Carefully, crack 1 egg into each well.
7. With a spoon, place some sauce over each egg and sprinkle with the remaining salt.
8. Place the feta around each egg evenly.
9. Place the skillet over low heat and cook, covered for about 5-7 minutes or until the desired doneness of the egg whites.
10. Now, transfer the skillet into the oven and broil for about 1 minute.
11. Remove from the oven and serve hot with the garnishing of cilantro.

## Eggs in Tomato Sauce

**Yield:** 6 servings
**Preparation Time:** 15 minutes
**Cooking Time:** 50 minutes

### Ingredients:

- 2 tablespoons butter
- 4 small yellow onions, sliced
- 1/3 cup sun-dried tomatoes, julienned
- 1 garlic clove, minced
- 6 large eggs
- 3 ounces feta cheese, crumbled
- Salt and freshly ground black pepper, to taste
- 2 tablespoons fresh parsley, chopped

### Instructions:

1. In a large cast iron skillet, melt the butter over medium-low heat and stir in the onions, spreading in an even layer.
2. Reduce the heat to low and cook for about 30 minutes, stirring after every 5-10 minutes.
3. Add the tomatoes and garlic and cook for about 2-3 minutes, stirring frequently.
4. With the spoon, spread the mixture in an even layer.
5. Carefully, crack the eggs over the onion mixture and sprinkle with the feta cheese, salt, and black pepper.
6. Cover the pan tightly and cook for about 10-15 minutes or until the desired doneness of the eggs.
7. Serve hot with the garnishing of the parsley.

## Eggs with Avocado

**Yield:** 6 servings
**Preparation Time:** 20 minutes
**Cooking Time:** 31 minutes

### Ingredients:

- 1 large avocado, peeled, halved and pitted
- Olive oil cooking spray
- 2-3 tablespoons feta cheese, crumbled
- 4 eggs, at room temperature
- Salt and freshly ground black pepper, to taste

### Instructions:

1. Preheat the oven to 400 degrees F.
2. Arrange 2 gratin dishes onto a baking sheet and place in the oven for about 10 minutes to heat up.
3. Cut each avocado half into 6 slices.
4. Remove the dishes from the oven spray with the cooking spray.
5. Arrange the avocado slices in each dish and very carefully, crack 2 eggs into each dish.
6. Sprinkle with feta, salt, and black pepper.
7. Bake for about 12-15 minutes or until the desired doneness of eggs.
8. Remove from the oven and serve hot.

## Tomato Omelet

**Yield:** 2 servings
**Preparation Time:** 10 minutes
**Cooking Time:** 5 minutes

### Ingredients:

- 4 large eggs
- A ¼ cup of water
- Salt and freshly ground black pepper, to taste
- 1 tablespoon butter
- ¼ cup goat cheese, crumbled
- ¼ cup tomato, chopped
- 1 scallion, chopped

### Instructions:

1. In a small bowl, add the eggs, water, salt, and black pepper and beat well.
2. In a large nonstick skillet, melt the butter over medium-high heat.
3. Add the egg mixture and cook for about 2 minutes.
4. Carefully, flip the omelet and cook for about 1-2 minutes or until set completely.
5. Place the cheese, tomato, and scallion over 1 side of the omelet.
6. Carefully, fold the omelet in half and remove from the heat.
7. Cut into 2 equal sized portions and serve.

## Veggie Omelet

**Yield:** 4 servings
**Preparation Time:** 15 minutes
**Cooking Time:** 15 minutes

### Ingredients:

- 1 teaspoon olive oil
- 2 cups fresh fennel bulbs, sliced thinly
- ¼ cup canned artichoke hearts, rinsed, drained and chopped
- ¼ cup green olives, pitted and chopped
- 1 Roma tomato, chopped
- 6 eggs
- Salt and freshly ground black pepper, to taste
- ½ cup goat cheese, crumbled

### Instructions:

1. Preheat the oven to 325 degrees F.
2. In a large ovenproof skillet, heat the oil over medium-high heat and sauté the fennel bulb for about 5 minutes.
3. Stir in the artichoke, olives, and tomato and cook for about 3 minutes.
4. Meanwhile, in a bowl, add the eggs, salt, and black pepper and beat until well combined.
5. Place the egg mixture over veggie mixture and stir to combine.
6. Cook for about 2 minutes.
7. Sprinkle with the goat cheese evenly and immediately, transfer the skillet into the oven.
8. Bake for about 5 minutes or until eggs is set completely.

9. Remove from oven and carefully transfer the omelet onto a cutting board.
10. Cut into desired size wedges and serve.

## Veggies & Egg Scramble

**Yield:** 2 servings
**Preparation Time:** 15 minutes
**Cooking Time:** 8 minutes

**Ingredients:**

- 1 tablespoon olive oil
- 1 cup fresh baby spinach
- 1/3 cup fresh tomato, chopped
- 3 eggs, beaten
- 2 tablespoons feta cheese, cubed
- Salt and freshly ground black pepper, to taste

**Instructions:**

1. In a large frying pan, heat the oil over medium heat and sauté the spinach and tomatoes for about 4 minutes.
2. Add the eggs and cook for about 1 minute, stirring continuously.
3. Stir in the feta and cook for about 2 minutes or until set.
4. Stir in the salt and black pepper and remove from the heat.
5. Serve immediately.

## Veggies & Chickpeas Hash

**Yield:** 4 servings
**Preparation Time:** 20 minutes
**Cooking Time:** 15 minutes

**Ingredients:**

- 2 tablespoons extra-virgin olive oil
- 2 russet potatoes, chopped
- 1 small onion, chopped
- 2 garlic cloves, chopped
- Salt and freshly ground black pepper, to taste
- 1 pound baby asparagus, trimmed and cut into ¼-inch pieces
- 1 cup low-sodium canned chickpeas, rinsed and drained
- 1 teaspoon dried oregano, crushed
- 1 teaspoon Za'atar
- 1 teaspoon ground allspice
- 1 teaspoon ground coriander
- 1 teaspoon paprika
- Pinch of sugar
- 1 teaspoon white vinegar
- 4 eggs
- 2 fresh Roma tomatoes, chopped
- 1 small red onion, chopped finely
- ½ cup fresh parsley, chopped
- ½ cup feta cheese, crumbled

**Instructions:**

1. In a large cast-iron skillet, heat the oil over medium-high heat and cook the potatoes,

yellow onion, garlic, salt, and black pepper for about 5-7 minutes, stirring frequently.
2. Stir in the asparagus, chickpeas, thyme, spices, sugar and a pinch of salt and black pepper and cook for about 6-8 minutes, stirring frequently.
3. Meanwhile, in a medium pan of the water, add the vinegar and bring to a simmer.
4. Crack the eggs, one at a time into a bowl and carefully slide into the pan of water.
5. Cook for about 3 minutes.
6. Carefully, remove the eggs from the water and place onto kitchen towel-lined plate to drain.
7. Sprinkle the eggs with the salt and black pepper.
8. Remove the potato hash from the heat and gently, stir in the tomatoes, onion, parsley and feta cheese.
9. Divide the hash mixture onto serving plates evenly.
10. Top each plate with 1 poached egg and serve.

### Spinach Frittata

**Yield:** 4 servings
**Preparation Time:** 15 minutes
**Cooking Time:** 20 minutes

**Ingredients:**

- 2 tablespoons extra-virgin olive oil
- 1 (5-ounce) package baby spinach
- 1 bunch scallions, sliced
- Salt and freshly ground black pepper, to taste

- 8 large eggs
- 4 tablespoons whole-wheat breadcrumbs, divided
- The ¾ cup of water
- ½ cup feta cheese, crumbled

**Instructions:**

1. Preheat the oven to 450 degrees F.
2. In a medium ovenproof skillet, heat the oil over medium-high heat and cook the spinach and scallions for about 4 minutes, stirring frequently.
3. Stir in the salt and black pepper and remove from the heat.
4. In a large bowl, add the eggs, 2 tablespoons of breadcrumbs, water and a ½ teaspoon of salt and beat until well combined.
5. Add the feta cheese and egg mixture into the skillet and mix well.
6. Spread the remaining breadcrumbs on top evenly.
7. Transfer the skillet into the oven and bake for about 15 minutes or until the top becomes golden.
8. Remove from the oven and set aside for about 5 minutes.
9. Cut the frittata into equal sized wedges and serve.

## Zucchini Frittata

**Yield:** 4 servings
**Preparation Time:** 15 minutes
**Cooking Time:** 20 minutes

**Ingredients:**

- 2 tablespoons almond milk

- 8 eggs
- Salt and freshly ground black pepper, to taste
- 1 tablespoon olive oil
- 1 garlic clove, minced
- 2 medium zucchinis, cut into ¼-inch thick round slices
- ½ cup goat cheese, crumbled

**Instructions:**

1. Preheat the oven to 350 degrees F.
2. In a bowl, add cup milk, eggs, salt, and black pepper and black pepper and beat well.
3. In an ovenproof skillet, heat oil over medium heat and sauté the garlic for about 1 minute.
4. Stir in the zucchini and cook for about 5 minutes.
5. Add the egg mixture and stir for about 1 minute.
6. Sprinkle the cheese on top evenly.
7. Immediately, transfer the skillet in the oven.
8. Bake for about 12 minutes or until eggs become set.
9. Remove from oven and set aside to cool for about 5 minutes.
10. Cut into desired size wedges and serve.

Are you enjoying this book?? I'd be REALLY HAPPY if you could leave a short review on Amazon, it means a lot to me! THANK YOU

# Lunch Recipes

### Tabbouleh

**Yield:** 3 servings
**Preparation Time:** 20 minutes

**Ingredients:**

- ½ cup uncooked bulgur
- 3 tablespoons olive oil, divided
- 2 cups boiling vegetable broth
- 2-3 fresh Roma tomatoes, cored and chopped
- 2-3 cups fresh Italian flat-leaf parsley, chopped
- ½ cup fresh mint, chopped
- ¼ cup scallions, chopped
- 2 tablespoons fresh lemon juice
- ½ teaspoon salt

**Instructions:**

1. In a large heat-proof bowl, add the bulgur and 1 tablespoon of the oil and mix well.
2. Pour hot broth and on top.
3. With a plastic wrap, cover the bowl tightly and set aside, covered for about 30-60 minutes or until softened.
4. Through a fine-mesh strainer, strain the bulgur.
5. In a large serving bowl, add the bulgur, 2 tablespoons of oil and remaining ingredients and mix until well combined.
6. Serve immediately.

## Cauliflower & Farro Salad

**Yield:** 4 servings
**Preparation Time:** 20 minutes
**Cooking Time:** 30 minutes

**Ingredients:**

**For Salad:**

- ¾ cup pearled farro
- Kosher salt, to taste
- 2 tablespoons olive oil
- 1 medium cauliflower head, cut into bite-sized florets
- ½ medium red onion, thinly sliced
- 1 ounce Parmesan cheese, shaved
- ¼ cup fresh parsley, chopped

**For Dressing:**

- 3 tablespoons extra-virgin olive oil
- 2 tablespoons fresh lemon juice
- 1 tablespoon tahini paste
- 1 small garlic clove, minced
- ½ teaspoon kosher salt

**Instructions:**

1. Heat a pan over medium heat toast the farro for about 4-5 minutes or until browned and nutty, shaking the pan occasionally.
2. Add the salt and enough water to cover the farro about 1-inch above and bring to a boil.

3. Cook for about 20-25 minutes or until tender but still chewy.
4. Through a fine mesh strainer, strain the farro.
5. Transfer the faro into a large bowl and set aside to cool slightly.
6. Meanwhile, the farro is cooking, in a skillet, heat the oil over medium-high heat and cook the cauliflower for about 5-6 minutes, stirring frequently.
7. Add the onion and sauté for about 2-3 minutes.
8. Remove from the heat and set aside.
9. For the dressing: in a bowl, add all the ingredients and beat until well combined.
10. In a large serving bowl, add the warm farro, cauliflower mixture and dressing and toss to coat well.
11. Serve with the garnishing of Parmesan cheese and parsley.

### Quinoa & Veggies Salad

**Yield:** 8 servings
**Preparation Time:** 20 minutes
**Cooking Time:** 20 minutes

**Ingredients:**

- 1½ cups dry quinoa, rinsed and drained
- 2½-3 cups water
- Kosher salt, to taste
- ½ cup extra-virgin olive oil
- 1 tablespoon balsamic vinegar
- 2 small garlic cloves, pressed

- ½ teaspoon dried thyme, crushed
- ½ teaspoon dried basil, crushed
- Freshly ground black pepper, to taste
- 3 cups fresh arugula
- 1 (15-ounce) can low-sodium garbanzo beans, rinsed and drained
- 1/3 cup fresh Kalamata olives, pitted and sliced
- 1/3 cup roasted red bell pepper, drained and chopped
- 1/3 cup feta cheese, crumbled
- ¼ cup fresh basil, slivered thinly

**Instructions:**

1. In a pan of the water, add the quinoa and ½ teaspoon of salt over high heat and bring to a boil.
2. Reduce the heat to low and cook, covered for about 15-20 minutes or until all liquid is absorbed.
3. Remove from the heat and with a fork, fluff the quinoa.
4. Set aside to cool completely.
5. For the dressing: in a bowl, add the oil, vinegar, garlic, dried herbs, salt, and black pepper and beat until well combined.
6. In a large serving bowl, add the quinoa, garbanzo beans, arugula, olives, bell pepper, and feta cheese and mix well.
7. Place the dressing over salad and toss to coat well.
8. Garnish with basil and serve.

## Chickpeas, Beans & Veggie Salad

**Yield:** 6 servings
**Preparation Time:** 20 minutes

**Ingredients:**

- 1 (15-ounce) can low-sodium chickpeas, rinsed and drained
- 1 (15-ounce) can low-sodium black beans, rinsed and drained
- 1 (15-ounce) can low-sodium corn, rinsed and drained
- 2 medium avocados, peeled, pitted and chopped
- 2 cups fresh cherry tomatoes, halved
- 1 (2¼-ounce) can diced olives, drained
- ¼ cup fresh cilantro, chopped
- 2 tablespoons extra-virgin olive oil
- 2 tablespoons fresh lime juice
- 1 teaspoon ground cumin
- ¼ teaspoon red chili powder
- ¼ teaspoon salt
- ¼ cup feta cheese, crumbled

**Instructions:**

1. In a large serving bowl, add the chickpeas, beans, corn, avocados, tomatoes, and olives and mix.
2. In a small bowl, add the remaining ingredients except for the feta cheese and beat until well combined.
3. Place the dressing over the salad and toss to coat well.
4. Serve with the garnishing of feta cheese.

## Asparagus, Arugula & Pasta Salad

**Yield:** 8 servings a
**Preparation Time:** 20 minutes
**Cooking Time:** 10 minutes

### Ingredients:

- 1 pound whole-wheat pasta
- 1 pound fresh asparagus, trimmed and into bite-sized pieces diagonally
- 1 tablespoon red wine vinegar
- 3 tablespoons fresh lemon juice
- 1-2 tablespoons lemon zest, grated
- 1 tablespoon olive oil
- 2 large handfuls fresh baby arugula
- ¼ cup fresh basil, julienned
- 2/3 cup feta cheese, crumbled
- ¼ cup pine nuts, toasted
- Freshly cracked black pepper, to taste

### Instructions:

1. In a large pan of the salted water, cook the pasta for about 8-10 minutes or until al dente or according to package's instructions.
2. In the last 3 minutes of the cooking, stir in the asparagus.
3. Remove from the heat and place the pasta and asparagus into a strainer to drain.
4. Rinse the pasta and asparagus under cold running water and drain well.
5. In the same pan, add the paste, asparagus, vinegar, oil, lemon juice, and lemon zest and toss to coat well.

6. Transfer the pasta mixture into a large serving bowl.
7. Add the arugula, basil, feta cheese, pine nuts, and a little black pepper and gently, toss to coat.
8. Serve immediately.

## Orzo & Veggie Salad

**Yield:** 6 servings
**Preparation Time:** 20 minutes
**Cooking Time:** 10 minutes

**Ingredients:**

**For Salad:**

- ½ cup uncooked orzo pasta
- 3 fresh plum tomatoes, chopped
- 1 cup marinated quartered artichoke hearts, chopped
- 1 cup fresh spinach, chopped roughly
- 2 scallions, chopped
- ½ cup feta cheese, crumbled
- 1 tablespoon capers, drained

**For Dressing:**

- 1/3 cup extra-virgin olive oil
- 4 teaspoons fresh lemon juice
- 1 tablespoon fresh tarragon, minced
- 2 teaspoons fresh lemon zest, grated
- 2 teaspoons rice vinegar

- ½ teaspoon salt
- ¼ teaspoon freshly ground black pepper

## Instructions:

1. In a large pan of the salted water, cook the orzo pasta for about 8-10 minutes or until al dente or according to package's instructions.
2. Drain the orzo and rinse under cold running water.
3. In a large serving bowl, add the pasta and remaining all salad ingredients and mix well.
4. For the dressing: in a small bowl, add all the ingredients and beat until well combined.
5. Place the dressing over salad and toss to coat well.
6. Refrigerate to chill completely before serving.

### Tuna, Beans & Veggies Salad

**Yield:** 4 servings
**Preparation Time:** 20 minutes
**Cooking Time:** 5 minutes

## Ingredients:

- ¾ pound green beans, trimmed and halved
- 1/3 cup water
- Salt, to taste
- 1 (12-ounce) can water-packed solid white Albacore tuna, drained
- 1 (16-ounce) can low-sodium Great Northern beans, drained and rinsed
- 1 (2¼-ounce) can sliced black olives, drained

- ¼ medium red onion, sliced thinly
- 6 tablespoons extra-virgin olive oil
- 3 tablespoons fresh lemon juice
- ½ teaspoon lemon zest, grated finely
- 1 teaspoon dried oregano
- Freshly ground black pepper, to taste
- 4 large hard-boiled eggs, peeled and quartered

**Instructions:**

1. In a pan, add the green beans, water and a large pinch of salt over high heat and bring to a boil.
2. Cook for about 5 minutes.
3. Remove from the heat and drain the green beans completely.
4. Immediately, place the green beans onto a paper towel-lined baking sheet to cool.
5. In a bowl, add the tuna, white beans, olives and onion, and mix.
6. In another bowl, add the oil, lemon juice, lemon zest, oregano, salt, and black pepper and beat until well combined.
7. Place the dressing over the salad and gently stir to combine.
8. Divide the tuna salad, green beans, and eggs onto serving plates and serve.

## Veggie Tortilla Wraps

**Yield:** 2 servings
**Preparation Time:** 20 minutes
**Cooking Time:** 5 minutes

### Ingredients:

- ½ teaspoon olive oil
- ½ small zucchini, sliced thinly
- ½ medium red bell pepper, seeded and sliced thinly
- 1 red onion, sliced thinly
- 2 whole grain tortillas
- ¼ cup hummus
- ½ cup fresh baby spinach
- 2 tablespoons feta cheese, crumbled
- 1 teaspoon dried oregano
- 1 tablespoon black olives, pitted and sliced

### Instructions:

1. In a small skillet, heat the oil over medium-low heat and sauté the zucchini, bell pepper, and onion for about 5 minutes.
2. Meanwhile, in another nonstick skillet, heat the tortilla, one at a time until warm.
3. Place the hummus onto the middle of each wrap evenly.
4. Top each tortilla with the spinach, followed by the sautéed vegetables, feta, oregano, and olives.
5. Carefully, fold the edges of each tortilla over the filling to roll up.
6. Cut each roll in half crosswise and serve.

## Lamb Filled Pita with Yogurt Sauce

**Yield:** 4 servings
**Preparation Time:** 15 minutes
**Cooking Time:** 6 minutes

### Ingredients:

- 2 garlic clove, minced
- 1 tablespoon fresh rosemary, minced
- Salt and freshly ground black pepper, to taste
- ¾ pound boneless leg of lamb, cut into bite-sized pieces
- 2 teaspoons olive oil
- 1 (6-ounce) container plat fat-free plain Greek yogurt
- 1½ cups cucumber, chopped finely
- 1 tablespoon fresh lemon juice
- 4 (6-ounce) whole-wheat pita bread, warmed

### Instructions:

1. In a bowl, add the garlic, rosemary, salt, and black pepper and mix well.
2. Add the lamb pieces and toss to coat well.
3. In a large nonstick skillet, heat the oil over medium-high heat.
4. Transfer the lamb mixture into the skillet and stir fry for about 4-6 minutes or until the desired the doneness of lamb.
5. Meanwhile for yogurt sauce in a bowl, mix together yogurt, cucumber, lemon juice, salt, and black pepper.
6. Transfer the lamb mixture between all the pitas evenly.

7. Serve immediately with the drizzling of the yogurt sauce.

## Grilled Veggie Sandwiches

**Yield:** 4 servings
**Preparation Time:** 25 minutes
**Cooking Time:** 5 minutes

**Ingredients:**

- Olive oil cooking spray
- ¼ cup mayonnaise
- ½ teaspoon fresh lemon juice
- 2 garlic cloves, minced
- 2 small zucchinis, sliced thinly lengthwise
- 1 eggplant, cut into ¼-inch thick slices
- 2 portabella mushrooms, cut into ¼-inch thick slices
- 2 tablespoons olive oil
- Salt, to taste
- ¾ of a ciabatta loaf, split horizontally
- ½ cup feta cheese, crumbled
- 2 medium tomatoes, cut into slices
- 2 cups fresh baby arugula

**Instructions:**

1. Preheat the grill to high heat. Grease the grill grate with the cooking spray.
2. In a bowl, add the mayonnaise, lemon juice, and garlic and mix well.

3. Set aside until using.
4. Coat the zucchini, eggplant, and mushrooms with oil evenly and then, sprinkle with salt.
5. Place the vegetable slices onto the grill and cook for about 1½ minutes per side.
6. Transfer the vegetable slices onto a plate.
7. Now, place the loaves onto the grill, cut side down and cook for about 2 minutes.
8. Remove from the grill and cut each loaf half into 4 equal sized pieces.
9. Spread the mayonnaise mixture over bottom of each bread piece evenly and top with the vegetable slices, followed by the tomatoes, arugula, and cheese.
10. Cover with top pieces and serve.


**Chicken Sandwiches with Aiolo**

**Yield:** 4 servings
**Preparation Time:** 20 minutes
**Cooking Time:** 15 minutes

**Ingredients:**

**For Aioli:**

- 1 (6½-ounce) jar marinated artichoke hearts, drained
- 2 tablespoons Parmesan cheese, grated
- 2 tablespoons mayonnaise
- 1 tablespoon fresh lemon juice
- ½ teaspoon fresh lemon zest, grated
- ¼ teaspoon red pepper flakes, crushed

- Salt and freshly ground black pepper, to taste

**For Sandwiches:**

- 4 (4-ounce) skinless, boneless chicken breast halves, cubed
- 1 tablespoon garlic, minced
- 1 tablespoon olive oil
- 1 teaspoon red pepper flakes, crushed
- Pinch of salt and freshly ground black pepper
- Olive oil cooking spray
- 1 red onion, chopped
- 1 yellow bell pepper, seeded and chopped
- ¼ cup capers, drained
- ¼ cup Kalamata olives, pitted and chopped
- 1 cup cherry tomatoes, halved
- ½ pound mozzarella cheese, shredded
- 1 cup feta cheese, crumbled
- 4 hoagie buns, split lengthwise and toasted
- ¼ cup fresh basil, chopped

**Instructions:**

1. For the aioli: in a food processor, add all the ingredients and pulse until smooth.
2. Transfer the aioli into a bowl.
3. Cover the bowl and refrigerate before serving.
4. For sandwiches: in a large bowl, add the chicken, garlic, oil, red pepper flakes, salt, and black pepper and toss to coat well.
5. Grease a large pan with the cooking spray and heat over medium-high heat.
6. Add the chicken cubes and cook the chicken mixture for about 5 minutes, stirring frequently.

7. Add the onion and bell pepper and cook for about 5 minutes.
8. Add the capers and olives and stir to combine.
9. Add the mozzarella cheese and stir until melted completely.
10. Remove from the heat and stir in the feta cheese.
11. Spread the aioli over each hoagie roll evenly.
12. Place the chicken mixture over the bottom half of each bun and top with the basil.
13. Cover with the top half of each bun and serve.

## Ham & Veggies Sandwich

**Yield:** 4 servings
**Preparation Time:** 20 minutes
**Cooking Time:** 2 minutes

**Ingredients:**

- 2 (3-ounce) ciabatta rolls, split
- Nonstick olive oil cooking spray
- ¼ cup light mayonnaise
- 1 teaspoon fresh lemon juice
- 1 tablespoon snipped fresh basil
- 1 cup fresh baby arugula
- 1-2 teaspoons white wine vinegar
- 4 ounces low-sodium cooked ham, sliced thinly
- 2 cups pears, cored and sliced thinly
- ¼ cup red onion, sliced thinly
- 1 ounce Parmesan cheese, shredded
- 1-2 teaspoons balsamic glaze

**Instructions**

1. Preheat the broiler of the oven on high. Arrange a rack about 4-5-inch from the heating element.
2. Arrange the rolls onto a baking sheet, cut side up and spray with the cooking spray.
3. Broil for about 1-2 minutes or until lightly toasted.
4. In a small bowl, add the mayonnaise, lemon juice, and basil and mix until well combined.
5. In another small bowl, add the arugula and vinegar and toss to coat well.
6. Spread the mayonnaise mixture onto each roll evenly.
7. Top each roll with ham slices, followed by the pears, arugula, onion, cheese, and balsamic glaze.
8. Serve immediately.

## Pita Pizza with Zucchini

**Yield:** 6 servings
**Preparation Time:** 15 minutes
**Cooking Time:** 5 minutes

**Ingredients:**

- 3 cups zucchini, shredded and squeezed
- ½ cup marble cheese, shredded
- 1/3 cup Parmesan cheese, grated
- 1 garlic clove, grated
- ½ teaspoon dried basil, crushed
- ½ teaspoon salt
- Freshly ground black pepper, to taste
- 6 whole wheat pitas
- Extra-virgin olive oil, as required

**Instructions:**

1. Preheat the broiler of oven. Line 2 large baking sheets with parchment paper.
2. In a bowl, add the zucchini, both kinds of cheese, garlic, basil, salt, and black pepper and mix well.
3. Arrange 3 pita bread onto each of prepared baking sheet.
4. Coat each pita bread with some oil and then top with zucchini mixture.
5. Broil for about 2-3 minutes or until edges become crisp and brown.
6. Now, transfer the baking sheets onto the lowest rack of the oven and broil for about 1-2 minutes or until cheese is melted.
7. With a pizza cutter, cut each pizza into 4 slices and serve.

## Pita Pizza with Shrimp

**Yield:** 1 serving
**Preparation Time:** 15 minutes
**Cooking Time:** 10 minutes

**Ingredients:**

- Olive oil cooking spray
- 2 tablespoons spaghetti sauce
- 1 tablespoon pesto sauce
- 1 (6-inch) pita bread
- 2 tablespoons mozzarella cheese, shredded
- 5 cherry tomatoes, halved
- 1/8 cup bay shrimp
- Pinch of garlic powder
- Pinch of dried basil

**Instructions:**

1. Preheat the oven to 325 degrees F. Lightly, grease a baking sheet with the cooking spray.
2. In a bowl, mix together the spaghetti sauce and pesto.
3. Spread the pesto mixture over the pita bread in a thin layer.
4. Top the pita bread with the cheese, followed by the tomatoes and shrimp.
5. Sprinkle with the garlic powder and basil.
6. Arrange the pita bread onto the prepared baking sheet and bake for about 7-10 minutes.
7. Remove from the oven and set aside for about 3-5 minutes before slicing.
8. Cut into desired sized slices and serve.

## Chicken & Veggies Flatbread Pizza

**Yield:** 4 servings
**Preparation Time:** 15 minutes
**Cooking Time:** 10 minutes

### Ingredients:

- 2 flatbreads
- 1 tablespoon Greek vinaigrette
- ½ cup feta cheese, crumbled
- ¼ cup Parmesan cheese, grated
- ½ cup water-packed artichoke hearts, rinsed, drained and chopped
- ½ cup black olives, pitted and sliced
- ½ cup cooked chicken breast strips, chopped
- 1/8 teaspoon dried basil, crushed
- 1/8 teaspoon dried oregano, crushed
- Pinch of ground black pepper
- 1 cup part-skim mozzarella cheese, shredded

### Instructions:

1. Preheat the oven to 400 degrees F.
2. Arrange the flatbreads onto a large ungreased baking sheet and coat each with vinaigrette.
3. Top each bread with the feta cheese, followed by the Parmesan, veggies, and chicken.
4. Sprinkle with the dried herbs and black pepper.
5. Top each bread with the mozzarella cheese evenly.
6. Bake for about 8-10 minutes or until cheese is melted.
7. Remove from the oven and set aside for about 1-2 minutes before slicing.
8. Cut each flatbread into 2 pieces and serve.

## Mixed Veggies Pizza

**Yield:** 5 servings
**Preparation Time:** 15 minutes
**Cooking Time:** 12 minutes

**Ingredients:**

- Olive oil cooking spray
- 1 (12-inch) prepared pizza crust
- ¼ teaspoon Italian seasoning
- ¼ teaspoon red pepper flakes, crushed
- 1 cup goat cheese, crumbled
- 1 (14-ounce) can quarter artichoke hearts
- 3 plum tomatoes, sliced into ¼-inch thick size
- 6 Kalamata olives, pitted and sliced
- ¼ cup fresh basil, chopped

**Instructions:**

1. Preheat the oven to 450 degrees F. Grease a baking sheet with the cooking spray.
2. Sprinkle the pizza crust with Italian seasoning and red pepper flakes evenly.
3. Place the goat cheese over crust evenly, leaving about ½-inch of the sides.
4. With the back of a spoon, gently press the cheese downwards.
5. Place the artichoke, tomato, and olives on top.
6. Place the pizza crust onto the prepared baking sheet.
7. Bake for about 10-12 minutes or until cheese becomes bubbly.
8. Remove from the oven and sprinkle with the basil.
9. Cut into equal sized wedges and serve.

## Beef & Veggie Pizza

**Yield:** 10 servings
**Preparation Time:** 25 minutes
**Cooking Time:** 50 minutes

**Ingredients:**

**For Crust:**

- 3 cups all-purpose flour
- 1 tablespoon sugar
- 2¼ teaspoons active dry yeast
- 1 teaspoon salt
- 2 tablespoons olive oil
- 1 cup of warm water
- Olive oil cooking spray

**For Topping:**

- 1 pound ground beef
- 1 medium onion, chopped
- 2 tablespoons tomato paste
- 1 tablespoon ground cumin
- Salt and freshly ground black pepper, to taste ¼ cup of water
- 1 cup fresh spinach, chopped
- 8 ounces artichoke hearts, quartered
- 4 ounces fresh mushrooms, sliced
- 2 fresh tomatoes, chopped
- 4 ounces feta cheese, crumbled

**Instructions:**

1. For the crust: in the bowl of a stand mixer, fitted with the dough hook, add the flour, sugar, yeast, and salt.
2. Add 2 tablespoons of the oil and warm water and knead until a smooth and elastic dough is formed.
3. Make a ball of the dough and set aside for about 15 minutes.
4. Place the dough onto a lightly floured surface and roll into a circle.
5. Lightly, grease a round pizza pan with the cooking spray.
6. Place the dough into the prepared pizza pan and gently, press to fit.
7. Set aside for about 10-15 minutes.
8. Now, coat the crust with some oil.
9. Preheat the oven to 400 degrees F.
10. For topping: heat a nonstick skillet over medium-high heat and cook the beef for about 4-5 minutes, stirring frequently.
11. Add the onion and cook for about 5 minutes, stirring frequently.
12. Add the tomato paste, cumin, salt, black pepper and water and stir to combine.
13. Reduce the heat to medium and cook for about 5-10 minutes.
14. Remove from the heat and set aside.
15. Place the beef mixture over the pizza crust and top with the spinach, followed by the artichokes, mushrooms, tomatoes, and Feta cheese.
16. Bake for about 25-30 minutes or until the cheese is melted.
17. Remove from the oven and set aside for about 3-5 minutes before slicing.
18. Cut into desired sized slices and serve.

## Falafel with Tahini Sauce

**Yield:** 8 servings
**Preparation Time:** 25 minutes
**Cooking Time:** 6 minutes

**Ingredients:**

**For Falafel:**

- 1 (15½-ounce) can low-sodium chickpeas, rinsed and drained
- 1 garlic clove, chopped
- ½ cup fresh parsley leaves, chopped roughly
- ¼ teaspoon ground cumin
- Salt and freshly ground black pepper, to taste
- ¼ cup all-purpose flour, divided
- 1 egg, beaten
- 2 tablespoons olive oil
- 8 cups lettuce leaves, torn

**For Tahini Sauce:**

- 4 large garlic cloves, minced
- ¼ cup fresh lemon juice
- ½ cup tahini
- ½ teaspoon fine sea salt
- Pinch of ground cumin
- 6 tablespoons of ice water

## Instructions:

1. For the falafel: in a food processor, add the chickpeas, garlic, parsley, cumin, salt, and black pepper and pulse until chopped.
2. Transfer the mixture into a bowl.
3. Add 2 tablespoons of the flour and egg and mix until well combined.
4. Make 8 equal sized patties from the mixture.
5. In a shallow dish, place the remaining flour.
6. Coat the patties with the roll evenly and then, shake off excess flour.
7. In a large nonstick skillet, heat the oil over medium-high heat and cook the patties for about 2-3 minutes per side or until golden browned.
8. Meanwhile, for tahini sauce: in a bowl, add the garlic and lemon juice and set aside for about 10 minutes.
9. Through a fine-mesh sieve, strain the garlic mixture into another medium bowl, pressing the garlic solids with a spatula to extract as much liquid as possible.
10. Then, discard the garlic.
11. In the bowl of the strained lemon juice, add the tahini, salt and cumin to and beat until well combined.
12. Slowly, add the water, 2 tablespoons at a time, beating well after each addition until smooth.
13. Divide the lettuce between serving plates evenly.
14. Place 2 patties onto each plate over lettuce.
15. Serve immediately with the drizzling of the tahini sauce.

## Lamb Koftas with Yogurt Sauce

**Yield:** 6 servings
**Preparation Time:** 20 minutes
**Cooking Time:** 10 minutes

**Ingredients:**

**For Lamb Kofta:**

- 1 pound ground lamb
- 2 tablespoons fat-free plain Greek yogurt
- 2 tablespoons onion, grated
- 2 teaspoons garlic, minced
- 2 tablespoons fresh cilantro, minced
- 1 teaspoon ground coriander
- 1 teaspoon ground cumin
- 1 teaspoon ground turmeric
- Salt and freshly ground black pepper, to taste
- 1 tablespoon olive oil

**For Yogurt Sauce:**

- ½ cup plain Greek yogurt
- ¼ cup roasted red bell pepper, chopped
- 2 teaspoons garlic, minced
- 1 teaspoon ground coriander
- 1 teaspoon ground cumin
- ½ teaspoon red pepper flakes, crushed
- Salt, to taste

**Instructions:**

1. For Koftas: in a large bowl, add all the ingredients and mix until well combined.
2. Make 12 equal sized oblong patties.
3. In a large nonstick skillet, heat oil medium-high heat.
4. Add the patties and cook for about 10 minutes or until browned from both sides, flipping occasionally.
5. Meanwhile, for the sauce: in a bowl, add all the ingredients and mix until well combined.
6. Serve the Koftas with the yogurt sauce.

## Chickpeas & Veggie Gazpacho

**Yield:** 10 servings
**Preparation Time:** 15 minutes

**Ingredients:**

- 1 (15½-ounce) can low-sodium chickpeas, rinsed and drained
- 1 large fresh plum tomato, chopped
- 1 large cucumber, peeled, seeded and chopped finely
- 1 celery stalk, chopped finely
- ½ of medium yellow bell pepper, seeded and chopped finely
- ½ of medium red bell pepper, seeded and chopped finely
- 2 tablespoons sweet onion, chopped finely
- 2 scallions, chopped

- 1 large garlic clove, minced
- ¼ cup fresh parsley, chopped
- 1 (46 fluid ounce) can low-sodium tomato juice
- 1 tablespoon fresh lemon juice
- Dash of hot pepper sauce
- 1 teaspoon curry powder
- Pinch of dried oregano, crushed
- Freshly ground black pepper, to taste
- ½ cup fresh parsley, chopped

**Instructions:**

1. In a large glass bowl, add all the ingredients except the parsley and gently stir to combine.
2. Cover the bowl tightly and refrigerate to chill for about 2 hours before serving.
3. Garnish with parsley and serve.

## Spicy Tomato Soup

**Yield:** 8 servings
**Preparation Time:** 15 minutes
**Cooking Time:** 28 minutes

**Ingredients:**

- 3 tablespoons olive oil
- 2 medium yellow onions, sliced thinly
- Salt, to taste
- 3 teaspoons curry powder

- 1 teaspoon ground cumin
- 1 teaspoon ground coriander
- ½ teaspoon red pepper flakes, crushed
- 1 (15-ounce) can low-sodium diced tomatoes with juice
- 1 (28-ounce) can low-sodium plum tomatoes with juices
- 5½ cups low-sodium vegetable broth
- ½ cup ricotta cheese, crumbled

**Instructions:**

1. In a Dutch oven, heat the oil over medium-low heat and cook the onion with 1 teaspoon of the salt for about 10-12 minutes, stirring occasionally.
2. Stir in the curry powder, cumin, coriander, and red pepper flakes and sauté for about 1 minute.
3. Stir in the tomatoes with juices and broth and simmer for about 15 minutes.
4. Remove from the heat and with a hand blender, blend the soup until smooth.
5. Serve immediately with the topping of ricotta cheese.

## Zucchini & Basil Soup

**Yield:** 6 servings
**Preparation Time:** 15 minutes
**Cooking Time:** 25 minutes

### Ingredients:

- 2 tablespoons olive oil
- 2½ pounds zucchini, chopped
- 1 medium onion, chopped
- 4 garlic cloves, chopped
- 4 cups chicken broth
- Salt and freshly ground black pepper, to taste
- 1/3 cup fresh basil leaves, chopped
- 2 tablespoons extra-virgin olive oil
- 1/3 cup heavy cream

### Instructions:

1. In a large pan, heat the olive oil over medium-low heat and cook the zucchini and onion for about 5-6 minutes, stirring frequently.
2. Add the garlic and cook for about 1 minute.
3. Add the chicken broth and bring to a boil over medium-high heat.
4. Reduce the heat to medium-low and simmer for about 15 minutes.
5. Stir in the basil, salt, and black pepper and remove from the heat.
6. With an immersion blender, blend the soup until smooth and creamy.
7. Divide the soup into serving bowls and drizzle with the extra-virgin olive oil.
8. Top with the cream and serve immediately.

## Veggies Soup

**Yield:** 8 servings
**Preparation Time:** 20 minutes
**Cooking Time:** 25 minutes

**Ingredients:**

- 8 carrots peeled and chopped
- 4 small zucchinis, chopped
- 4 small onions, chopped
- 2 (14-ounce) cans low-sodium diced tomatoes with juice
- 1 leek, chopped
- 2 garlic cloves, minced
- 1 teaspoon ground cumin
- ¼ teaspoon ground cayenne pepper
- ¼ teaspoon paprika
- Salt and freshly ground black pepper, to taste
- 4¼ cups vegetable broth
- 1 wholemeal bread slice, toasted and cut up into small croutons

**Instructions:**

1. In a large soup pan, add all the ingredients except the croutons and over high heat and bring to a boil.
2. Reduce the heat to low and simmer, partially covered for about 20 minutes.
3. Remove from the heat and set aside to cool slightly.
4. In a blender add the soup in batches and pulse until smooth.

5. Return the pureed mixture into the same pan over medium heat and simmer for about 3-4 minutes.
6. Remove from the heat and serve hot with the topping of croutons.

### Chickpeas Stew

**Yield:** 3 servings
**Preparation Time:** 15 minutes
**Cooking Time:** 35 minutes

**Ingredients:**

- 1 tablespoon extra-virgin olive oil
- 1 red bell pepper, seeded and julienned
- 3 scallions, sliced thinly
- 1 jalapeño pepper, chopped
- 2 garlic cloves, minced
- ½ teaspoon ground cumin
- ½ teaspoon paprika
- 1 (28-ounce) can low-sodium whole, peeled tomatoes, crushed
- Pinch of brown sugar
- Salt and ground black pepper, as required
- ½ cup low-sodium vegetable broth
- 2 cups low-sodium canned chickpeas, rinsed and drained
- 2 tablespoons fresh parsley, minced
- 1 teaspoon fresh lemon zest, grated

**Instructions:**

1. In a pan, heat the oil over medium heat and sauté the bell pepper, scallions, jalapeño, garlic, pan, cumin, and paprika for about 4-5 minutes.
2. Stir in the tomatoes, brown sugar, salt, black pepper, and broth and bring to a boil.
3. Reduce the heat to medium-low and simmer for about 20 minutes.
4. Stir in the chickpeas, parsley and lemon zest and simmer for about 10 minutes.
5. Remove from the heat and serve hot.

## Vegetable Curry

**Yield:** 6 servings
**Preparation Time:** 20 minutes
**Cooking Time:** 30 minutes

**Ingredients:**

- 6 tablespoons olive oil, divided
- 2 carrots, peeled and chopped
- 1 sweet potato, peeled and cubed
- 1 medium eggplant, cubed
- 1 red bell pepper, seeded and chopped
- 1 green bell pepper, seeded and chopped
- 1 onion, chopped
- 3 garlic cloves, minced
- 1 tablespoon curry powder
- 1 teaspoon ground turmeric
- 1 teaspoon ground cinnamon
- ¾ teaspoon ground cayenne pepper
- ¾ tablespoon of sea salt

- 1 (15-ounce) can low-sodium garbanzo beans, rinsed and drained
- 1 zucchini, sliced
- 1 cup fresh orange juice
- ¼ cup blanched almonds
- 2 tablespoons golden raisins
- 10 ounces fresh spinach

**Instructions:**

1. In a large Dutch oven, heat 3 tablespoons of the oil over medium heat and sauté the carrots, sweet potato, eggplant, bell peppers, and onion for about 5 minutes.
2. Meanwhile, in another medium frying pan, heat the remaining oil over medium heat and sauté the garlic, curry powder, cinnamon, turmeric, cayenne pepper, and salt for about 3 minutes.
3. Transfer the garlic mixture into the pan of the vegetables and stir to combine.
4. Stir in the beans, zucchini, orange juice, almonds and raisins and simmer, covered for about 20 minutes.
5. Stir in the spinach and cook, uncovered for about 5 minutes.
6. Remove from the heat and serve hot.

## Couscous with Cauliflower & Dates

**Yield:** 4 servings
**Preparation Time:** 20 minutes
**Cooking Time:** 40 minutes

**Ingredients:**

- 2 cups cauliflower florets
- 4 tablespoons olive oil, divided
- Salt and freshly ground black pepper, to taste
- 2 garlic cloves, minced
- 1¼ cups vegetable broth
- 1 cup pearl couscous
- 1 tablespoon fresh lemon juice
- 1 shallot, chopped
- 3 tablespoons dates, pitted and chopped
- 1 teaspoon red wine vinegar
- 2 tablespoons fresh parsley, chopped

**Instructions:**

1. Preheat the oven to 400 degrees F. Line a baking sheet with parchment paper.
2. Ina bowl, add the cauliflower florets, 2 tablespoons of the oil, salt and black pepper and toss to coat well.
3. Transfer the cauliflower florets onto the prepared baking sheet and spread in an even layer.
4. Roast for about 35-40 minutes or until the cauliflower is golden.
5. Remove the cauliflower from the oven and set aside to cool for about 10 minutes.

6. Meanwhile, for couscous: in a large pan, heat 1 tablespoon of the oil on medium-high heat and sauté the garlic for about 1 minute.
7. Add the broth and bring to a boil.
8. Stir in couscous and reduce the heat to medium.
9. Cover the pan and simmer for about 8-10 minutes or until done completely, stirring occasionally.
10. Stir in the lemon juice and remove from the heat.
11. Meanwhile, in a skillet, heat the remaining oil over medium heat and sauté the shallot for about 6 minutes.
12. Stir in the dates and cook for about 2 minutes.
13. Stir in the vinegar, salt, and black pepper and remove from the heat.
14. Transfer the date mixture into the pan with the couscous and stir to combine.
15. Remove from the heat and set aside to cool slightly.
16. In a large serving bowl, add the couscous and cauliflower and gently stir to combine.
17. Serve warm with the garnishing of parsley.

## Chicken & Veggie Kabobs

**Yield:** 8 servings
**Preparation Time:** 20 minutes
**Cooking Time:** 10 minutes

**Ingredients:**

- ¼ cup white vinegar
- ¼ cup fresh lemon juice
- ¼ cup olive oil
- 2 garlic cloves, minced
- ½ teaspoon dried thyme, crushed
- ½ teaspoon dried oregano, crushed
- 1 teaspoon ground cumin
- Salt and freshly ground black pepper, to taste
- 2 pounds skinless, boneless chicken breast, cubed into ½-inch size
- Olive oil cooking spray
- 1 medium red bell pepper, seeded and cubed into 1-inch size
- 1 medium green bell pepper, seeded and cubed into 1-inch size
- 1 zucchini, sliced
- 16 fresh mushrooms, sliced
- 16 cherry tomatoes
- 1 large onion, quartered and separated into pieces

**Instructions:**

1. In a large bowl, add the vinegar, lemon juice, oil, garlic, dried herbs, cumin, salt, and black pepper and mix until well combined.

2. Add the chicken cubes and coat with the mixture generously.
3. Refrigerate, covered to marinate for about 2-4 hours.
4. Preheat the outdoor grill to medium-high heat. Grease the grill grate with the cooking spray.
5. Remove the chicken from the bowl and discard the excess marinade.
6. Thread the chicken and vegetables onto pre-soaked wooden skewers respectively.
7. Place the skewers onto the grill and cook for about 10 minutes or until the desired doneness, flipping occasionally.
8. Remove from the grill and serve hot.

## Chicken & Grape Kebabs

**Yield:** 4 servings
**Preparation Time:** 25 minutes
**Cooking Time:** 10 minutes

### Ingredients:

- 1/3 cup extra-virgin olive oil, divided
- 2 garlic cloves, minced
- 1 tablespoon fresh rosemary, minced
- 1 tablespoon fresh oregano, minced
- 1 teaspoon fresh lemon zest, grated
- ½ teaspoon red chili flakes, crushed
- 1 pound boneless, skinless chicken breast, cut into ¾-inch cubes
- Olive oil cooking spray
- 1¾ cups California green seedless grapes, rinsed

## Grilled Prawns with Garlic Sauce

**Yield:** 8 servings
**Preparation Time:** 20 minutes
**Cooking Time:** 17 minutes

**Ingredients:**

**For Garlic Sauce:**

- 2 small garlic heads, top trimmed off
- 2 cups fresh cilantro leaves, chopped
- 4 tablespoons fresh lime juice
- 2 tablespoons dry white wine
- ½ cup extra-virgin olive oil
- 3 tablespoons chili paste

**For Prawns:**

- Olive oil cooking spray
- 3¼ pounds large prawns, peeled and deveined, with tails intact
- 6 large garlic cloves, minced
- 1/3 cup extra-virgin olive oil
- 2 tablespoons fresh lemon juice
- Salt and freshly ground black pepper, to taste

**Instructions:**

1. Preheat the oven to 400 degrees F.
2. For garlic sauce: trim the top of the garlic head to expose a bit of the clove, but keep intact.
3. Drizzle the garlic heads with the olive oil generously.

- ½ teaspoon salt
- 1 tablespoon fresh lemon juice

**Instructions:**

1. In a small bowl, add a ¼ cup of the oil, garlic, fresh herbs, lemon zest, and chili flakes and beat until well combined.
2. Thread the chicken cubes and grapes onto 12 metal skewers.
3. In a large baking dish, arrange the skewers.
4. Place the marinade and mix well.
5. Refrigerate to marinate for about 4-24 hours.
6. Preheat the grill to medium-high heat. Grease the grill grate with the cooking spray.
7. Remove the skewers from baking dish and shake off the excess marinade.
8. Now, sprinkle the skewers with the salt.
9. Place the skewers onto the grill and cook for about 3-5 minutes per side or until chicken is done completely.
10. Remove from the grill and transfer the skewers onto a serving platter.
11. Drizzle with lemon juice and remaining oil and serve.

4. With a piece of the foil, wrap the garlic heads.
5. Roast for about 10-15 minutes or until slightly tender and fragrant.
6. Remove the garlic heads from the oven and set aside, uncovered to cool slightly.
7. Peel each garlic head and place into a bowl.
8. With a fork, crush the roasted garlic finely.
9. In the bowl of garlic, add the remaining sauce ingredients and beat until well combined.
10. Set aside until using.
11. Preheat the barbecue grill to high heat. Lightly, grease the grill grate with the cooking spray.
12. For prawns: in a bowl, add all the ingredients and toss to coat well.
13. Place the prawns onto the grill and cook for about 1 minute per side.
14. Remove from the grill and transfer the prawns onto serving plates.
15. Serve alongside the garlic sauce.

**Octopus in Honey Sauce**

**Yield:** 8 servings
**Preparation Time:** 20 minutes
**Cooking Time:** 1 hour 25 minutes

**Ingredients:**

- 2¼ pounds fresh octopus washed
- 1 bay leaf
- 1/3 cup water
- 4 tablespoons olive oil
- 2 onions, chopped finely

- Pinch of saffron threads, crushed
- 1 garlic clove, chopped finely
- 1 tablespoon tomato paste
- 1 (14-ounce) can low-sodium diced tomatoes
- 1 tablespoon honey
- ¾ cup red wine
- Salt and freshly ground black pepper, to taste
- ¼ cup fresh basil leaves, chopped

**Instructions:**

1. Remove the eyes of the octopus and cut out the beak.
2. Then, clean the head thoroughly.
3. In a deep pan, add the octopus, bay leaf and water over medium heat and cook for about 20 minutes.
4. Add the wine and simmer for about 50 minutes.
5. Meanwhile, for the sauce: in a skillet, heat the oil over medium heat and sauté the onions and saffron for about 3-4 minutes.
6. Add the garlic and tomato paste and sauté for about 1-2 minutes.
7. Stir in the tomatoes and honey and simmer for about 10 minutes.
8. Transfer the sauce into the pan of octopus and cooking for about 15 minutes.
9. Serve hot with the garnishing of basil.

## Mussels in Wine & Tomato Sauce

**Yield:** 6 servings
**Preparation Time:** 20 minutes
**Cooking Time:** 12 minutes

## Ingredients:

- 1 tablespoon olive oil
- 2 celery stalks, chopped
- 1 onion, chopped
- 4 garlic cloves, minced
- ½ teaspoon dried oregano, crushed
- 1 (15-ounce) can low-sodium tomatoes, chopped
- 1 teaspoon honey
- 1 teaspoon red pepper flakes, crushed
- 2 pounds mussels, cleaned
- 2 cups white wine
- Salt and freshly ground black pepper, to taste
- ¼ cup fresh basil leaves, chopped

## Instructions:

1. In a skillet, heat the oil over medium heat and sauté the celery, onion, and garlic for about 5 minutes.
2. Add the tomato, honey, and red pepper flakes and simmer for about 10 minutes.
3. Meanwhile, in a large pan, add the mussels and wine and bring to a boil.
4. Simmer, covered for about 10 minutes.
5. Transfer the mussel mixture into tomato mixture and stir to combine.
6. Season with salt and black pepper and remove from heat.

7. Serve hot with the garnishing of basil.

## Pasta with Tomatoes & Herbs

**Yield:** 4 servings
**Preparation Time:** 15 minutes
**Cooking Time:** 15 minutes

**Ingredients:**

- 8 ounces angel hair pasta
- 2 tablespoons olive oil
- 1 tablespoon garlic, minced
- 1 tablespoon dried oregano, crushed
- 1 tablespoon dried basil, crushed
- 1 teaspoon dried thyme, crushed
- 2 cups cherry tomatoes, halved

**Instructions:**

1. In a large pan of the lightly salted boiling water, add the pasta and cook for about 8-10 minutes or according to package's instructions.
2. Drain the pasta well.
3. In a large skillet, heat the oil over medium heat and sauté the garlic for about 1 minute.
4. Stir in herbs and sauté for about 1 minute more.
5. Add the pasta and cook for about 2-3 minutes or until heated completely.
6. Fold in tomatoes and remove from the heat.
7. Serve hot.

## Pasta with Mushrooms

**Yield:** 6 servings
**Preparation Time:** 15 minutes
**Cooking Time:** 20 minutes

### Ingredients:

- 3 tomatoes
- 1 pound pasta (of your choice)
- ¼ cup olive oil
- 1 pound fresh mushrooms, sliced
- 3 garlic cloves, minced
- 1 teaspoon dried oregano, crushed
- 1 (2-ounce) can black olives, drained
- ¾ cup feta cheese, crumbled

### Instructions:

1. In a large pan of the salted boiling water, add the tomatoes and cook for about 1 minute.
2. With a slotted spoon, transfer the tomatoes into a bowl of ice water.
3. In the same pan of the boiling water, add the pasta and cook for about 8-10 minutes.
4. Drain the pasta well.
5. Meanwhile, peel the blanched tomatoes and then chop them.
6. In a large skillet, heat oil over medium heat and sauté the mushrooms and garlic for about 4-5 minutes.
7. Add the tomatoes and oregano and cook for about 3-4 minutes.

8. Divide the pasta onto serving plates and top with mushroom mixture.
9. Garnish with olives and feta and serve.

## Pasta with Veggies

**Yield:** 6 servings
**Preparation Time:** 20 minutes
**Cooking Time:** 45 minutes

**Ingredients:**

- 1 tablespoon olive oil
- 1 large sweet onion, chopped finely
- 2 medium carrots, peeled and chopped finely
- ½ pound fresh baby Portobello mushrooms, chopped finely
- 1 large zucchini, chopped finely
- 3 garlic cloves, minced
- ½ cup dry red wine
- 1 (28-ounce) can low-sodium crushed tomatoes with juices
- 1 (14½-ounces) can low-sodium diced tomatoes with juices
- ½ cup Parmesan cheese, grated
- ½ teaspoon dried oregano, crushed
- ½ teaspoon freshly ground black pepper
- 1/8 teaspoon red pepper flakes, crushed
- Pinch of ground nutmeg
- 4½ cups uncooked whole-wheat Rigatoni

**Instructions:**

1. In a large pan, heat the oil over medium-high heat and sauté the carrots and onion for about 4-5 minutes.
2. Add the mushrooms, zucchini, and garlic and cook and for about 5-6 minutes.
3. Stir in the wine and bring to a boil.
4. Cook for about 2-3 minutes or until all the liquid is absorbed.
5. Stir in the tomatoes, cheese, oregano, and spices and bring to a boil.
6. Reduce the heat to low and simmer, covered for about 25-30 minutes or until the desired thickness.
7. Meanwhile, in a large pan of the salted water, add the rigatoni and cook for about 8-10 minutes or until al dente or according to package's instructions.
8. Drain the rigatoni well.
9. Transfer the rigatoni onto serving plates evenly.
10. Top with the veggie sauce and serve.

# Mediterranean Diet For Beginners

## Pasta with Shrimp & Spinach

**Yield:** 4 servings
**Preparation Time:** 15 minutes
**Cooking Time:** 10 minutes

**Ingredients:**

- 1 cup sour cream
- ½ cup feta cheese, crumbled
- 3 garlic cloves, chopped
- 2 teaspoons dried basil, crushed
- ¼ teaspoon red pepper flakes, crushed
- 8 ounces uncooked pasta (of your choice)
- 1 (10-ounce) packages frozen spinach, thawed
- 12 ounces medium shrimp, peeled and deveined
- Salt and freshly ground black pepper, to taste

**Instructions:**

1. In a large serving bowl, add the sour cream, feta, garlic, basil, red pepper flakes, and salt and mix well.
2. Set aside until using.
3. In a large pan of the lightly salted boiling water, add the fettuccine and cook for about 10 minutes or according to the package's Instructions.
4. In the last 2 minutes, stir in the spinach and shrimp.
5. Drain the pasta mixture well.
6. Add the hot pasta mixture into the bowl of the sour cream mixture and gently, toss to coat.
7. Serve immediately.

## Rigatoni with Salmon

**Yield:** 8 servings
**Preparation Time:** 20 minutes
**Cooking Time:** 20 minutes

### Ingredients:

- Olive oil cooking spray
- 1 pound boneless salmon fillets
- Salt and freshly ground black pepper, to taste
- 16 ounces uncooked whole-wheat Rigatoni
- ½ cup fresh basil leaves, chopped finely
- 2 teaspoons capers
- 1 teaspoon garlic, minced
- 2 teaspoons fresh lemon zest, grated finely
- 2 tablespoons fresh lemon juice
- 2 tablespoons extra-virgin olive oil
- ¼ cup Parmesan cheese, grated

### Instructions:

1. Preheat the oven to 350 degrees F. Grease a baking sheet with the cooking spray.
2. Season the salmon fillet with salt and pepper evenly.
3. Arrange the salmon fillet onto the prepared baking sheet.
4. Bake for about 15-20 minutes or until the desired doneness.

5. Remove from the oven and with a fork, flake the salmon into bite-sized pieces.
6. Meanwhile, in a large pan of the salted water, add the rigatoni and cook for about 8-10 minutes or until al dente or according to package's instructions.
7. Drain the rigatoni and transfer into a bowl.
8. Add the remaining ingredients except for the Parmesan and toss to coat well.
9. Add the flaked salmon and gently, toss to coat well.
10. Serve immediately with the garnishing of parmesan cheese.

# Dinner Recipes

### Spicy Lentil Soup

**Yield:** 6 servings
**Preparation Time:** 20 minutes
**Cooking Time:** 1¼ hours

**Ingredients:**

- tablespoons olive oil
- 2 carrots, peeled and chopped
- 2 celery stalks, chopped
- 2 sweet onions, chopped
- 3 garlic cloves, minced
- 1½ cups brown lentils picked over and rinsed
- 1 (14½-ounce) can low-sodium diced tomatoes
- ¼ teaspoon dried basil, crushed
- ¼ teaspoon dried oregano, crushed
- ¼ teaspoon dried thyme, crushed
- 1 teaspoon ground cumin
- ½ teaspoon ground coriander
- ½ teaspoon paprika
- 6 cups low-sodium vegetable broth
- 3 cups fresh spinach, chopped
- Salt and freshly ground black pepper, to taste
- 2 tablespoons fresh lemon juice

**Instructions:**

1. In a large soup pan, heat the oil over medium heat and sauté carrot, celery, and onion for about 4-5 minutes.
2. Add the garlic, sauté for about 1 minute.
3. Add the lentils and sauté for about 2-3 minutes.
4. Stir in the tomatoes, herbs, spices, and broth and bring to a boil.
5. Reduce the heat to low and simmer, partially covered for about 45-60 minutes.
6. Stir in the spinach, salt, and black pepper and cook for about 3-4 minutes.
7. Stir in the lemon juice and serve hot.

## Chicken & Pasta Soup

**Yield:** 8 servings
**Preparation Time:** 20 minutes
**Cooking Time:** 35 minutes

**Ingredients:**

- 2 tablespoons olive oil
- 1½ pounds skinless, boneless chicken breasts, cubed into ¾-inch size
- 1 tablespoon Greek seasoning
- Salt and freshly ground black pepper, to taste
- 1 large onion, chopped finely
- 1 carrot, peeled and chopped
- 1 garlic clove, minced
- ¼ cup white wine
- ¼ cup sun-dried tomatoes, chopped

- 1 tablespoon capers, drained
- 1½ teaspoons fresh oregano, minced
- 1½ teaspoons fresh basil, minced
- 7 cups low-sodium chicken broth
- 1½ cups uncooked pasta (of your choice)
- 2 tablespoons fresh lemon juice
- 2 teaspoons fresh parsley, chopped finely

**Instructions:**

1. In a Dutch oven, heat the oil over medium heat and cook the chicken breasts with Greek seasoning, salt, and black pepper for about 4-5 minutes or until golden brown from both sides.
2. With a slotted spoon, transfer the chicken breasts onto a plate and set aside.
3. In the same pan, add the scallions and garlic and sauté for about 1 minute.
4. Add the wine and remove the scrape the brown bits from the bottom of the pan.
5. Stir in the cooked chicken, tomatoes, capers, oregano, basil and broth and bring to a boil.
6. Reduce the heat to low and simmer, covered for about 15 minutes.
7. Increase the heat to medium and again bring to a boil.
8. Stir in the pasta and cook for about 8-10 minutes or until the desired doneness of the pasta.
9. Stir in the lemon juice and parsley and remove from the heat.
10. Serve hot.

## Lamb, Lentils & Chickpeas Soup

**Yield:** 8 servings
**Preparation Time:** 20 minutes
**Cooking Time:** 2¼ hours

### Ingredients:

- 1½ pounds boneless lamb shoulder, cubed
- Salt and freshly ground black pepper, to taste
- 2 tablespoons olive oil
- 1 onion, chopped
- 2 garlic cloves, chopped
- 2 tablespoons tomato paste
- 2 teaspoons sweet paprika
- 1½ teaspoons ground cumin
- ½ teaspoon ground cloves
- 2 (14-ounce) cans low-sodium diced tomatoes
- 4 cups low-sodium chicken broth
- 2 (14-ounce) cans low-sodium brown lentils, rinsed and drained
- 2 (14-ounce) cans low-sodium chickpeas, rinsed and drained
- ½ cup fresh parsley, chopped

### Instructions:

1. Season the lamb cubes with salt and black pepper evenly.
2. In a large pan, heat the oil over medium-high heat and sear the lamb cubes in 2 batches for about 4-5 minutes.
3. With a slotted spoon, transfer the lamb cubes into a bowl.

4. In the same pan, add the onion and garlic over medium heat and sauté for about 3-4 minutes.
5. Add the cooked lamb, tomato paste and spices and cook for about 1 minute.
6. Stir in the tomatoes and broth and bring to a boil.
7. Reduce the heat to low and simmer, covered for about 1 hour.
8. Stir in the lentils and chickpeas and simmer, covered for about 30 minutes.
9. Uncover and simmer for about 30 minutes more.
10. Stir in the salt and black pepper and remove from the heat.
11. Serve hot with the garnishing of parsley.

**Cannellini Beans & Farro Stew**

**Yield:** 6 servings
**Preparation Time:** 20 minutes
**Cooking Time:** 45 minutes

**Ingredients:**

- 2 tablespoons olive oil
- 1 cup carrots, peeled and chopped
- 1 cup celery, chopped
- 1 cup yellow onion, chopped
- 4 garlic cloves, minced
- 1 (14½-ounce) can diced tomatoes
- 1 cup uncooked farro, rinsed
- ½ cup fresh parsley sprigs
- 1 bay leaf
- 1 teaspoon dried oregano
- Salt, to taste

- 5 cups low-sodium vegetable broth
- 4 cups fresh kale, thick ribs removed and chopped
- 1 (15-ounce) can low-sodium cannellini beans, rinsed and drained
- 1 tablespoon fresh lemon juice
- ½ cup feta cheese, crumbled

**Instructions:**

1. In a large pan, heat the oil over medium-high heat and sauté the carrots, celery, and onion for about 3 minutes.
2. Add the garlic and sauté for about 30 seconds.
3. Stir in the tomatoes, farro, parsley sprigs, bay leaf, oregano, salt, and broth and bring to a boil.
4. Reduce the heat to medium-low and simmer covered for about 20 minutes.
5. With a slotted spoon, remove the parsley sprigs and discard them.
6. Stir in the kale and cook for about 10-15 minutes or until the desired doneness.
7. Stir in the cannellini beans and cook for about 3-5 minutes or until heated completely.
8. With a slotted spoon, remove the bay leaf and discard it.
9. Stir in the lemon juice and remove from the heat.
10. Serve hot with the topping of feta cheese.

## Quinoa, Beans and Vegetables Stew

**Yield:** 6 servings
**Preparation Time:** 20 minutes
**Cooking Time:** 45 minutes

**Ingredients:**

- 3 tablespoons extra-virgin olive oil
- 1-2 cups seasonal vegetables (zucchini, yellow squash, bell pepper, sweet potatoes), chopped
- 3 carrots, peeled and chopped
- 2 celery stalks, chopped
- 1 medium yellow onion, chopped
- Salt, to taste
- 6 garlic cloves, minced
- ½ teaspoon dried thyme, crushed
- 1 (28-ounce) can low-sodium diced tomatoes with juices
- 1 cup quinoa, rinsed and drained
- 4 cups low-sodium vegetable broth
- 2 cups of water
- 2 bay leaves
- Pinch of red pepper flakes, crushed
- Freshly ground black pepper, to taste
- 1 (15-ounce) can low-sodium Great Northern beans, rinsed and drained
- 1 cup fresh kale, tough ribs removed and chopped
- 1-2 teaspoons fresh lemon juice
- ¼ cup Parmesan cheese, grated freshly

**Instructions:**

1. In a large Dutch oven, heat the oil over medium heat and cook the seasonal vegetables, carrots, celery, onion and a pinch of salt for about 6-8 minutes, stirring occasionally.
2. Add the garlic and thyme and cook for about 1 minute, stirring frequently.
3. Stir in the diced tomatoes with juices and cook for about 2-3 minutes, stirring occasionally.
4. Add the quinoa, broth, water, bay leaves, red pepper flakes, 1 teaspoon of salt and black pepper and stir to combine.
5. Increase the heat to high and bring to a boil.
6. Reduce the heat to low and simmer, partially covered for about 25 minutes.
7. Stir in the beans and kale and simmer, uncovered for about 5 minutes.
8. Remove from the heat and discard the bay leaves.
9. Stir in the lemon juice and serve hot with the topping of Parmesan cheese.

### Beef & Prunes Stew

**Yield:** 8 servings
**Preparation Time:** 20 minutes
**Cooking Time:** 1 hour 35 minutes

**Ingredients:**

- 1 tablespoon olive oil
- 2 pounds boneless beef chuck roast, cut into ¾-inch cubes

- 1 (14½-ounce) can low-sodium diced tomatoes with juice
- ¼ cup quick-cooking tapioca
- 1 tablespoon organic honey
- 2 teaspoons ground cinnamon
- ¼ teaspoon garlic powder
- Salt and freshly ground black pepper, to taste
- ¼ cup red wine vinegar
- 2 cups beef broth
- 3 cups sweet potato, peeled and cubed
- 2 medium yellow onions, cut into thin wedges
- 2 cups prunes, pitted

**Instructions:**

1. In a Dutch oven, heat 1 tablespoon of the oil over medium-high heat and sear the beef cubes in 2 batches for about 4-5 minutes or until browned.
2. Drain off the grease from the pan.
3. Stir in the tomatoes, tapioca, honey, cinnamon, garlic powder, black pepper, vinegar, and broth and bring to a boil.
4. Reduce the heat to low and simmer, covered for about 1 hour, stirring occasionally.
5. Stir in the onions and sweet potato and simmer, covered for about 20-30 minutes.
6. Stir in the prunes and cook for about 3-5 minutes.
7. Remove from the heat and serve hot.

## Seafood & Tomato Stew

**Yield:** 4 servings
**Preparation Time:** 20 minutes
**Cooking Time:** 25 minutes

### Ingredients:

- 2 tablespoons extra-virgin olive oil
- 1 medium onion, chopped finely
- 2 garlic cloves, minced
- ¼ teaspoon red pepper flakes, crushed
- ½ pound plum tomatoes, seeded and chopped
- 1/3 cup white wine
- 1 cup clam juice
- 1 tablespoon tomato paste
- Salt, to taste
- 1 pound snapper fillets, cubed into 1-inch size
- 1 pound large shrimp, peeled and deveined
- ½ pound sea scallops
- 1/3 cup fresh parsley, minced
- 1 teaspoon fresh lemon zest, grated finely

### Instructions:

1. In a large Dutch oven, heat the oil over medium heat and sauté the onion for about 3-4 minutes.
2. Add the garlic and red pepper flakes and sauté for about 1 minute.
3. Add the tomatoes and cook for about 2 minutes.
4. Stir in the wine, clam juice, tomato paste, and salt and bring to a boil.
5. Reduce the heat to low and simmer, covered for about 10 minutes.

6. Stir in the seafood and simmer, covered for about 6-8 minutes.
7. Stir in the parsley and remove from heat.
8. Serve hot with the garnishing of lemon zest.

## Roasted Whole Chicken

**Yield:** 4 servings
**Preparation Time:** 15 minutes
**Cooking Time:** 1 hour 35 minutes

**Ingredients:**

- ¼ cup extra-virgin olive oil
- 3 garlic cloves, minced
- 2 teaspoons fresh lemon zest, grated finely
- 2 teaspoons dried oregano, crushed
- 1 teaspoon paprika
- 1 teaspoon ground cayenne pepper
- 1 teaspoon ground cumin
- ½ teaspoon ground fennel seeds
- Salt and freshly ground black pepper, to taste
- 1 (3-pound) frying chicken, neck, and giblets removed

**Instructions:**

1. In a large bowl, add all the ingredients except the chicken and mix well.
2. Add the chicken and coat with the mixture generously.
3. Refrigerate to marinate overnight, turning occasionally.

4. Preheat the oven to 425 degrees F.
5. Remove the chicken from the bowl and arrange in a roasting pan.
6. Coat the chicken with marinade.
7. With a kitchen string, tie the legs and tuck the wings back under the body.
8. Roast for about 10 minutes.
9. Now, reduce the temperature of the oven to 350 degrees F and roast for about 1½ hours.
10. Remove from the oven and place the chicken onto a cutting board for about 10 minutes before carving.
11. With a sharp knife, cut the chicken into desired sized pieces and serve.

**Lemony Chicken Breasts with Yogurt Sauce**

**Yield:** 4 servings
**Preparation Time:** 20 minutes
**Cooking Time:** 12 minutes

**Ingredients:**

**For Yogurt Sauce:**

- 1 garlic clove, minced
- 1 cup fresh dill, stems removed and chopped
- 1¼ cups plain Greek yogurt
- 1 tablespoon olive oil
- 1 tablespoon fresh lime juice
- Pinch ground cayenne pepper
- Salt, to taste

**For Chicken Breast:**

- 4 (4-ounce) boneless, skinless chicken breast halves
- 3 garlic cloves, chopped finely
- 3 tablespoons fresh parsley, chopped
- 3 tablespoons olive oil
- 3 tablespoons fresh lemon juice
- 1 teaspoon paprika
- ½ teaspoon dried oregano
- Salt and freshly ground black pepper, to taste
- Olive oil cooking spray

**Instructions:**

1. For the yogurt sauce: in a food processor, add all the ingredients and pulse until all the ingredients are well combined and smooth.
2. Transfer the sauce into a small bowl.
3. Cover the bowl and refrigerate until using.
4. For chicken breasts: with a fork, pierce chicken breasts several times.
5. In a large bowl, add all the ingredients except the chicken breasts and mix until well combined.
6. Add the chicken breasts and coat with the marinade generously.
7. Refrigerate to marinate for about 2-3 hours.
8. Preheat the grill to medium-high heat. Grease the grill grate with the cooking spray.
9. Remove the chicken from bowl and shake off excess marinade.
10. Place the chicken breasts onto the grill and cook for about 5-6 minutes per side.
11. Remove from the grill and transfer the chicken breasts onto the serving plate.
12. Serve hot alongside the yogurt sauce.

## Chicken Breasts with Balsamic Fig Sauce

**Yield:** 4 servings
**Preparation Time:** 15 minutes
**Cooking Time:** 20 minutes

**Ingredients:**

- 4 (6-ounce) skinless, boneless chicken breast halves
- 1½ tablespoons fresh thyme leaves, chopped and divided
- ½ teaspoon salt, divided
- ¼ teaspoon freshly ground black pepper
- 2 tablespoons olive oil, divided
- ¾ cup onion, chopped
- ½ cup dried figs, chopped finely
- ½ cup low-fat, low-sodium chicken broth
- ¼ cup balsamic vinegar
- 2 teaspoons low-sodium soy sauce

**Instructions:**

1. In a small bowl, add 1½ teaspoons of thyme, a ¼ teaspoon of salt and black pepper and mix well.
2. Season the chicken breast halves with the thyme mixture evenly.
3. In a large nonstick skillet, heat 1 tablespoon of the oil over medium-high heat and cook the chicken for about 6 minutes per side or until done completely.
4. With a slotted spoon, transfer the chicken onto a plate and with a piece of foil, cover them to keep warm.

5. In the same skillet, heat the remaining oil over medium heat and sauté the onion for about 3 minutes.
6. Stir in the figs, broth, vinegar and soy sauce and simmer for about 3 minutes.
7. Stir in the remaining thyme and salt and remove from the heat.
8. Cut the chicken breast halves into slices diagonally.
9. Serve the chicken slices with the topping of fig sauce.

## Bruschetta Chicken Breasts

**Yield:** 4 servings
**Preparation Time:** 15 minutes
**Cooking Time:** 40 minutes

**Ingredients:**

- Olive oil cooking spray
- 4 (4-6-ounce) chicken breasts
- Salt and freshly ground black pepper, to taste
- 5 small tomatoes, chopped
- ¼ cup fresh basil leaves, chopped
- 1 garlic clove, minced
- 1 teaspoon balsamic vinegar
- 1 teaspoon olive oil

**Instructions:**

1. Preheat the oven to 375 degrees F. Grease a baking dish with the cooking spray.

2. Season the chicken breasts with the salt and black pepper evenly.
3. Arrange the chicken breasts into the prepared baking dish in a single layer.
4. Cover the baking dish and bake for about 35-40 minutes or until chicken is done completely.
5. Meanwhile, in a bowl, add the tomatoes, basil, garlic, vinegar, oil and salt mix well.
6. Refrigerate until using.
7. Remove from the oven and transfer the chicken breasts onto the serving plates.
8. Top with tomato mixture and serve.

### Chicken with Caper Sauce

**Yield:** 2 servings
**Preparation Time:** 15 minutes
**Cooking Time:** 15 minutes

**Ingredients:**

- ½ cup all-purpose flour
- Sea salt, to taste
- 2 (6-ounce) skinless, boneless chicken breast halves
- 2 tablespoons extra-virgin olive oil
- ¼ cup dry white wine
- 3 tablespoons fresh lime juice
- ¼ cup cold unsalted butter, cut into pieces
- 2 tablespoons capers, drained
- ½ lime, cut into wedges

## Instructions:

1. In a shallow dish, add the flour and salt and mix well.
2. Add the chicken breasts and coat with the flour mixture evenly.
3. Then, shake off the excess.
4. In a skillet, heat the oil over medium-high heat and cook the chicken breasts for about 3-4 minutes per side.
5. With a slotted spoon, transfer the chicken breasts onto a plate and with a piece of foil, cover them to keep warm.
6. In the same skillet, add the wine and bring to a boil, scraping up the browned bits from the bottom of the pan.
7. Add the lemon juice and cook for about 2-3 minutes or until reduced by half.
8. Add the butter and cook until the sauce becomes thick, shaking the pan vigorously.
9. Remove from the heat and stir in the capers.
10. Place the caper sauce over the chicken and serve with lime wedges.

## Braised Chicken with Artichokes

**Yield:** 4 servings
**Preparation Time:** 20 minutes
**Cooking Time:** 1¼ hours

### Ingredients:

- 1 tablespoon olive oil
- 4 chicken leg quarters
- 1 Yellow onion, chopped
- 4 garlic cloves, chopped
- 1 teaspoon salt
- 1 tablespoon freshly ground black pepper
- ½ teaspoon red pepper flakes, crushed
- 4 cups low-sodium chicken broth
- 10 canned artichoke hearts, drained and halved
- 2 cups cherry peppers
- 8 fresh thyme sprigs
- 4 tablespoons fresh lemons juice
- 1 (16-ounce) can low-sodium butter beans, rinsed and drained

### Instructions:

1. Preheat the oven to 375 degrees F.
2. In a Dutch oven, heat the oil over high heat and sear the chicken for about 5 minutes per side.
3. With a slotted spoon, transfer the chicken onto a warm plate.
4. In the same pan, add the onion, garlic, salt, black pepper, and red pepper flakes and sauté for about 1 minute.
5. Stir in the broth and bring to a boil.

6. Remove from the heat and stir in the cooked chicken, artichoke hearts, cherry peppers, thyme sprigs, and lemon juice.
7. Cover the pan and transfer into the oven.
8. Bake for about 1 hour.
9. Remove from the oven and with a slotted spoon, transfer the chicken onto a warm plate.
10. Add the beans into the pan and stir to combine.
11. Divide chicken leg quarters into the serving bowls and top with the artichoke mixture.
12. Serve immediately.

### Chicken & Dried Fruit Casserole

**Yield:** 4 servings
**Preparation Time:** 20 minutes
**Cooking Time:** 50 minutes

**Ingredients:**

- 6 ounces dried apricots, quartered
- 6 ounces dried prunes, quartered
- 4 ounces black olives, pitted
- 2 ounces capers
- 2 garlic cloves, crushed
- 2 tablespoons fresh oregano, minced
- Salt and freshly ground black pepper, to taste
- 1 bay leaf
- 2/3 cup red wine vinegar
- ¼ cup olive oil
- 4 (6-ounce) chicken drumsticks
- 3 tablespoons brown sugar
- ¾ cup white wine

## Instructions:

1. For the marinade: in a large baking dish, add the apricots, prunes, olives, capers, garlic, oregano, salt, black pepper, bay leaf, vinegar and oil, and mix until well combined.
2. Add the chicken breasts and coat with the marinade generously.
3. Cover the baking dish and refrigerate, covered overnight.
4. Remove from the refrigerator and set aside in the room temperature for at least 1 hour before cooking.
5. Preheat the oven to 325 degrees F.
6. Remove the chicken breasts from the bowl and arrange in a baking dish in a single layer.
7. Spread the marinade over the chicken breasts evenly and sprinkle with the brown sugar.
8. Place the white wine around the chicken breasts.
9. Bake for about 50 minutes.
10. Remove from the oven and serve hot.

### Steak with Yogurt Sauce

**Yield:** 6 servings
**Preparation Time:** 20 minutes
**Cooking Time:** 15 minutes

**Ingredients:**

**For Steak:**

- Olive oil cooking spray

- 3 garlic cloves, minced
- 2 tablespoons fresh rosemary, chopped
- Salt and freshly ground black pepper, to taste
- 2 pounds flank steak, trimmed

**For Sauce:**

- 1½ cups fat-free plain Greek yogurt
- 1 cucumber, peeled, seeded and chopped finely
- 1 cup fresh parsley, chopped
- 1 garlic clove, minced
- 1 teaspoon fresh lemon zest, grated finely
- 1/8 teaspoon ground cayenne pepper
- Salt and freshly ground black pepper, to taste

**Instructions:**

1. Preheat the grill to medium-high heat. Grease the grill grate with the cooking spray.
2. For the steak: in a large bowl, add all the ingredients except the steak and mix until well combined.
3. Coat the steak with the mixture generously.
4. Set aside for about 15 minutes.
5. Place the steak onto the grill and cook for about 12-15 minutes, flipping after every 3-4 minutes.
6. Remove from the grill and place the steak onto a cutting board for about 5 minutes.
7. Meanwhile, for the sauce: in a bowl, add all the ingredients and mix well.
8. With a sharp knife, cut the steak into desired sized slices.
9. Serve the steak slices with the topping of yogurt sauce.

## Beef & Olives Bake

**Yield:** 6 servings
**Preparation Time:** 20 minutes
**Cooking Time:** 2¼ hours

**Ingredients:**

- 2 tablespoons olive oil
- 1 pound 10 ounces lean stewing steak, cut into large chunks
- 2 red onions, cut into thick wedges
- 3 bell peppers, seeded and cut into thick slices
- 1¼ pounds plum tomatoes, quartered
- 2 tablespoons sun-dried tomato paste
- 5 ounces canned green olives, drained
- 1/3 cup fresh oregano, chopped
- 2 heads garlic, halved
- 1 cup red wine
- ½ cup of water
- Salt and freshly ground black pepper, to taste

**Instructions:**

1. Preheat the oven to 375 degrees F.
2. In a roasting pan, heat the oil over medium heat and sear the steak chunks in 2 batches for about 5 minutes or until browned.
3. With a slotted spoon, transfer the steak chunks into a bowl.
4. In the same roasting pan, add the onions and bell peppers and sauté for about 5 minutes.
5. Add the cooked steak chunks and remaining ingredients and stir to combine.

6. With a piece of the foil, cover the roasting tin and bake for about 1 hour.
7. Remove the foil and bake for about 1 hour more.
8. Remove from the oven and serve hot.

## Leg of Lamb with Potatoes

**Yield:** 8 servings
**Preparation Time:** 20 minutes
**Cooking Time:** 1¼ hours

**Ingredients:**

**For Lamb & Potatoes:**

- 1 (4-pound) bone-in leg of lamb, fat trimmed
- Salt and freshly ground black pepper, to taste
- 5 garlic cloves, sliced
- 8 medium potatoes, peeled and cut into wedges
- 1 medium onion, peeled and cut into wedges
- 1 teaspoon garlic powder
- 1 teaspoon paprika
- 2 cups of water

**For Spice Mixture:**

- ½ cup olive oil
- ¼ cup fresh lemon juice
- 5 garlic cloves, peeled
- 2 tablespoons dried mint
- 2 tablespoons dried oregano
- 1 tablespoon paprika

- ½ tablespoon ground nutmeg

**Instructions:**

1. Remove the leg of lamb from the refrigerator and set aside at room temperature for about 1 hour before cooking.
2. For spice mixture: in a food processor, add all the ingredients and pulse until smooth.
3. Transfer the spice mixture into a bowl and set aside.
4. Preheat the broiler of the oven.
5. With paper towels, pat dries the leg of lamb completely.
6. With a sharp knife, make a few slits on both sides the leg of lamb and season with salt and black pepper.
7. Place the leg of lamb onto a wire rack and arrange the rack over the top oven rack.
8. Broil for about 5-7 minutes per side.
9. Remove from the oven and transfer the leg of lamb onto a platter to cool slightly.
10. Now, set the oven temperature to 375 degrees F. Arrange a rack in the middle of the oven.
11. Place a wire rack into a large roasting pan.
12. Carefully, insert the garlic slices in the slits of the leg of the lamb and rub with spice mixture generously.
13. In a bowl, add the potato, onion, garlic powder, paprika, and a little salt and toss to coat well.
14. Place 2 cups of water into the bottom of the prepared roasting pan

15. Place the leg of lamb in the middle of the prepared roasting pan and arrange the potato and onion wedges around the lamb.
16. With a large piece of foil, cover the roasting pan.
17. Roast for about 1 hour.
18. Remove the foil and roast for about 10-15 minutes more.
19. Remove from the oven and place the leg of lamb onto a cutting board for at least 20 minutes before carving.
20. Cut into desired sized slices and serve alongside potatoes.

**Veggies & Feta Stuffed Leg of Lamb**

**Yield:** 10 servings
**Preparation Time:** 20 minutes
**Cooking Time:** 1 hour 40 minutes

**Ingredients:**

- 1/3 cup fresh parsley, minced
- 8 garlic cloves, minced and divided
- 3 tablespoons extra-virgin olive oil, divided
- Salt and freshly ground black pepper, to taste
- 1 (4-pound) boneless leg of lamb, butterflied and trimmed
- 1/3 cup yellow onion, minced
- 1 bunch fresh kale, trimmed and chopped
- ½ cup Kalamata olives, pitted and chopped
- ½ cup feta cheese, crumbled
- 1 teaspoon fresh lemon zest, finely grated
- Olive oil cooking spray

## Instructions:

1. In a large baking dish, add the parsley, 4 garlic cloves, 2 tablespoons of oil, salt, and black pepper and mix until well combined.
2. Add the leg of lamb and generously coat with parsley mixture.
3. Set aside at room temperature.
4. In a large skillet, heat the remaining oil over medium heat and sauté the onion and remaining garlic for about 4-5 minutes.
5. Add the kale and cook for about 4-5 minutes.
6. Remove from the heat and set aside to cool for at least 10 minutes.
7. After cooing, stir in the remaining ingredients.
8. Preheat the oven to 450 degrees F. Grease a shallow roasting pan with the cooking spray.
9. Place the leg of lamb onto a smooth surface, cut-side up.
10. Place the kale mixture in the center of the leg of lamb, leaving 1-inch border from both sides.
11. Roll the short side to seal the stuffing and with a kitchen string, tightly tie the roll at many places.
12. Arrange the roll into the prepared roasting pan, seam-side down.
13. Roast for about 15 minutes.
14. Now, adjust the temperature of the oven to 350 degrees F.
15. Roast for about 1-1¼ hours.
16. Remove the leg of lamb from oven and place onto a cutting board for about 10-20 minutes before slicing.
17. With a sharp knife, cut the roll into desired size slices and serve.

## Spiced Lamb Chops

**Yield:** 8 servings
**Preparation Time:** 15 minutes
**Cooking Time:** 8 minutes

**Ingredients:**

- 1 tablespoon fresh mint leaves, chopped
- 1 teaspoon garlic paste
- 1 teaspoon ground allspice
- ½ teaspoon ground nutmeg
- ½ teaspoon ground green cardamom
- ¼ teaspoon hot paprika
- Salt and freshly ground black pepper, to taste
- 4 tablespoons olive oil
- 2 tablespoons fresh lemon juice
- 2 racks of lamb chops, trimmed and separated into 16 chops
- 2 tablespoons unsalted butter
- 4½ cups fresh cherry tomatoes

**Instructions:**

1. In a large bowl, add all the ingredients except the chops, butter, and tomatoes and mix until well combined.
2. Add the chops and coat with the mixture generously.
3. Refrigerate to marinate for about 5-6 hours.
4. Preheat the gas grill to high heat. Grease the grill grate.

5. Place the lamb chops onto the grill and cook for about 6-8 minutes, flipping once halfway through.
6. Serve hot.
7. Meanwhile, in a skillet, melt the butter over medium heat and cook the tomatoes with some salt for about 1-2 minutes, stirring frequently.
8. Remove the lamb chops from the grill and divide onto the serving plates.
9. Serve alongside the tomatoes.

## Lamb Chops with Herbed Pistachios

**Yield:** 4 servings
**Preparation Time:** 20 minutes
**Cooking Time:** 8 minutes

**Ingredients:**

**For Lamb Chops:**

- ½ teaspoon ground coriander
- ½ teaspoon ground cumin
- 1/8 teaspoon ground cinnamon
- Salt and freshly ground black pepper, to taste
- 8 (4-ounce) lamb loin chops, trimmed
- 1 tablespoon olive oil
- 6 cups fresh baby spinach

**For Pistachio Topping:**

- 2 tablespoons pistachios, chopped finely

- 1 garlic clove, minced
- 2 teaspoons fresh lemon peel, grated finely
- 1½ tablespoons fresh cilantro, chopped
- 1½ tablespoons fresh parsley, chopped
- Salt, to taste

**Instructions:**

1. In a large bowl, add the spices, salt, and black pepper and mix well.
2. Add lamb chops and coat with spice mixture generously.
3. In a large skillet, heat the oil over medium-high heat and sear the chops for about 4 minutes per side or until the desired doneness.
4. Meanwhile, for topping: in a bowl, add all the ingredients and mix well.
5. Remove the chops from the heat and divide onto the serving plates.
6. Top the chops with the pistachio mixture and serve alongside the spinach.

## Lamb Chops with Veggies

**Yield:** 4 servings
**Preparation Time:** 20 minutes
**Cooking Time:** 27 minutes

### Ingredients:

- 8 (4-ounce) lamb loin chops
- ½ cup fresh basil leaves
- ½ cup fresh mint leaves
- 1 tablespoon fresh rosemary leaves
- 2 garlic cloves
- 3 tablespoons olive oil
- 2 zucchinis, sliced
- 1 red bell pepper, seeded and cut into large chunks
- 1 eggplant, sliced
- 1¾ ounces feta cheese, crumbled
- 8 ounces fresh cherry tomatoes

### Instructions:

1. Preheat the oven to 390 degrees F.
2. In a food processor, add the fresh herbs, garlic and 2 tablespoons of the oil and pulse until smooth.
3. Transfer the herb mixture into a large bowl.
4. Add the lamb chops and coat with the herb mixture evenly.
5. Refrigerate to marinate for about 2-3 hours.
6. In the bottom of a large baking sheet, place the zucchini, bell pepper, and eggplant slices and drizzle with the remaining oil.
7. Arrange the lamb chops on top in a single layer.
8. Bake for about 20 minutes.

9. Remove from the oven and transfer the chops onto a platter.
10. With a piece of foil, cover the chops to keep warm.
11. Now, place the cherry tomatoes into the baking sheet with veggies and top with the feta cheese.
12. Bake for about 5-7 minutes or until the cheese just starts to become golden brown.
13. Serve the chops alongside the vegetables.

**Pork Chops with Balsamic Peach Glaze**

**Yield:** 2 servings
**Preparation Time:** 15 minutes
**Cooking Time:** 23 minutes

**Ingredients:**

- 2 bone-in pork chops
- Kosher salt and freshly ground black pepper, to taste
- 2 tablespoons extra-virgin olive oil
- ½ cup balsamic vinegar
- 1 tablespoon honey
- 1 tablespoon fresh oregano, chopped
- 2 peaches, pitted and sliced
- 6 ounces feta cheese, crumbled
- ½ cup fresh basil, chopped
- Crushed red pepper flakes, to taste

**Instructions:**

1. Preheat the broiler of the oven to high.

2. Season the pork chops with the salt and black pepper evenly.
3. In a large ovenproof skillet, heat the oil over medium-high heat and sear the pork chops for about 3-4 minutes per side.
4. Reduce the heat to medium and cook for about 6-8 minutes.
5. In a small bowl, add the balsamic vinegar, honey, and oregano and beat until well combined.
6. Stir in the vinegar mixture and cook for about 2 minutes.
7. Remove from the heat and stir in the peaches.
8. Transfer the skillet to the oven and broil for about 4-5 minutes or until the peaches are lightly charred.
9. Remove from the oven and serve hot with the topping of feta, basil and chili flakes.

### Baked Fish with Tomatoes & Capers

**Yield:** 6 servings
**Preparation Time:** 15 minutes
**Cooking Time:** 38 minutes

**Ingredients:**

- 1/3 cup extra-virgin olive oil
- 1 small red onion, chopped finely
- 2 large tomatoes, chopped
- 1/3 cup golden raisins
- 10 garlic cloves, chopped
- 1½ tablespoons capers
- 1½ teaspoons ground coriander

- 1 teaspoon ground cumin
- 1 teaspoon sweet Spanish paprika
- ½ teaspoon ground cayenne pepper
- Salt and freshly ground black pepper, to taste
- 1½ pounds white fish fillets
- 1 tablespoon fresh lemon juice
- 1 teaspoon fresh lemon zest, grated finely
- Chopped fresh parsley, for garnishing

**Instructions:**

1. Preheat the oven to 400 degrees F.
2. In a medium pan, heat the oil over medium-high heat and sauté the onion for about 3 minutes.
3. Add the tomatoes, raisins, garlic, capers, spices, a pinch of salt and black pepper and bring to a boil.
4. Reduce the heat to medium-low and simmer for about 15 minutes.
5. Meanwhile, season the fish fillets with the salt and black pepper evenly.
6. Remove the pan from the heat and place about ½ of the cooked tomato sauce in the bottom of a 9½x13-inch baking dish evenly.
7. Place the fish fillets over sauce and top with the lemon juice, lemon zest, and remaining tomato sauce.
8. Bake for about 15-18 minutes or until fish is done completely.
9. Remove from the oven and serve hot with the garnishing of parsley.

## Salmon with Avocado Cream

**Yield:** 4 servings
**Preparation Time:** 15 minutes
**Cooking Time:** 8 minutes

**Ingredients:**

**For Avocado Cream:**

- 2 medium ripe avocados, peeled, pitted and chopped
- 1 cup low-fat plain Greek yogurt
- 2 garlic cloves, chopped
- 3-4 tablespoons fresh lime juice
- Salt and freshly ground black pepper, to taste

**For Salmon:**

- 2 teaspoons ground cumin
- 2 teaspoons red chili powder
- 2 teaspoons paprika
- 2 teaspoons garlic powder
- Salt and freshly ground black pepper, to taste
- 4 (6-ounce) skinless salmon fillets
- 2 tablespoons unsalted butter

**Instructions:**

1. For avocado cream: in a food processor, add all the ingredients and pulse until smooth.
2. For salmon: in a small bowl, add the spices, salt, and black pepper and mix well.

3. Coat the salmon fillets with the spice mixture evenly.
4. In a nonstick skillet, melt the butter over medium-high heat and cook the salmon fillets for about 3 minutes.
5. Flip and cook for about 4-5 minutes or until the desired doneness of the salmon.
6. Transfer the salmon fillets onto the serving plates.
7. Top with avocado cream and serve.

## Salmon with Fennel & Couscous

**Yield:** 4 servings
**Preparation Time:** 20 minutes
**Cooking Time:** 22 minutes

**Ingredients:**

- 1¼ pounds boneless, skinless salmon, cut into 4 equal sized portions
- ¼ teaspoon salt
- ¼ teaspoon freshly ground black pepper
- 4 tablespoons sun-dried tomato pesto, divided
- 2 tablespoons extra-virgin olive oil, divided
- 2 medium fennel bulbs, cut into ½-inch wedges and fronds reserved
- 1 cup whole-wheat couscous
- 3 scallions, sliced thinly
- ¼ cup green olives, pitted and sliced
- 2 tablespoons pine nuts, toasted
- 2 garlic cloves, sliced
- 2 teaspoon fresh lemon zest, grated finely
- 1½ cups low-sodium chicken broth

- 1 lemon, cut into 8 slices

**Instructions:**

1. Season the salmon prices with the salt and black pepper evenly.
2. The spread 1½ teaspoons of the pesto on each salmon piece evenly.
3. In a large skillet, heat 1 tablespoon of the oil over medium-high heat and cook half of the fennel for about 2-3 minutes or until brown on the bottom.
4. With a slotted spoon, transfer the fennel onto a plate.
5. Repeat with the remaining oil and fennel.
6. In the same skillet, add the couscous and scallions over medium heat and cook or about 1-2 minutes or lightly toasted, stirring frequently.
7. Add the olives, pine nuts, garlic, lemon zest, remaining 2 tablespoons of the pesto and broth and stir to combine.
8. Place the cooked fennel and salmon on top and gently, press into the couscous mixture.
9. Arrange the lemon slices on top evenly.
10. Reduce the heat to medium-low and cook, covered for about 10-14 minutes or until the desired doneness of the salmon and couscous.
11. Remove from the heat and serve hot with the topping of reserved fennel fronds.

## Grilled Salmon

**Yield:** 4 servings
**Preparation Time:** 15 minutes
**Cooking Time:** 12 minutes

**Ingredients:**

- ½ cup low-sodium plain Greek yogurt
- 3 garlic cloves, minced
- 2 tablespoons fresh dill, minced
- 2 tablespoons fresh lemon juice
- 1 tablespoon extra-virgin olive oil
- 1½ teaspoons ground coriander
- 1½ teaspoons ground cumin
- Salt and freshly ground black pepper, to taste
- 4 (6-ounce) skinless salmon fillets
- Olive oil cooking spray
- 2 tablespoons fresh basil leaves

**Instructions:**

1. In a large bowl, add all the ingredients except the salmon and basil and mix until well combined.
2. Transfer half of the yogurt mixture into another bowl and reserve in refrigerator for serving.
3. In the large bowl of the remaining yogurt mixture, add the salmon fillets and coat with the mixture well.
4. Refrigerate for about 25-30 minutes, flipping once halfway through.
5. Preheat the grill to medium-high heat. Lightly, grease the grill grate with the cooking spray.

6. Remove the salmon fillets from the bowl and with the paper towels, discard the excess yogurt mixture.
7. Place the salmon fillets onto the grill and cook for about 4-6 minutes per side.
8. Remove from the grill and transfer the salmon fillets onto the serving plates.
9. Garnish with the basil and serve with the topping of the reserved yogurt mixture.

**Cod in Spicy Tomato Sauce**

**Yield:** 5 servings
**Preparation Time:** 15 minutes
**Cooking Time:** 35 minutes

**Ingredients:**

- 1 teaspoon dried dill weed
- 2 teaspoons sumac
- 2 teaspoons ground coriander
- 1½ teaspoons ground cumin
- 1 teaspoon ground turmeric
- 2 tablespoons extra-virgin olive oil
- 1 large sweet onion, chopped
- 8 garlic cloves, chopped
- 2 jalapeño peppers, chopped
- 5 medium tomatoes, chopped
- 3 tablespoons tomato paste
- 2 tablespoons fresh lime juice
- ½ cup of water
- Salt and freshly ground black pepper, to taste
- 5 (6-ounce) boneless cod fillets

**Instructions:**

1. For spice mixture: in a small bowl, add the dill weed and spices and mix well.
2. In a large, deep skillet, heat the oil over medium-high heat and sauté the onion for about 2 minutes.
3. Add the garlic and jalapeno and sauté for about 2 minutes.
4. Stir in the tomatoes, tomato paste, lime juice, water, half of the spice mixture, salt and pepper and bring to a boil.
5. Reduce the heat to medium-low and cook, covered for about 10 minutes, stirring occasionally.
6. Meanwhile, season the cod fillets with the remaining spice mixture, salt, and pepper evenly.
7. Place the fish fillets into the skillet and gently, press into the tomato mixture.
8. Increase the heat to medium-high and cook for about 2 minutes.
9. Reduce the heat to medium and cook, covered for about 10-15 minutes or until the desired doneness of the fish.
10. Remove from the heat and serve hot.

## Halibut Parcel with Olives & Capers

**Yield:** 4 servings
**Preparation Time:** 15 minutes
**Cooking Time:** 40 minutes

### Ingredients:

- 1 onion, chopped
- 1 large tomato, chopped
- 1 (5-ounce) jar pitted Kalamata olives
- ¼ cup capers
- ¼ cup olive oil
- 1 tablespoon fresh lemon juice
- Salt and freshly ground black pepper, to taste
- 4 (6-ounce) halibut fillets
- 1 tablespoon Greek seasoning

### Instructions:

1. Preheat the oven to 350 degrees F.
2. In a bowl, add the onion, tomato, onion, olives, capers, oil, lemon juice, salt, and black pepper and mix well.
3. Season the halibut fillets with the Greek seasoning evenly.
4. Arrange the halibut fillets onto a large piece of foil.
5. Top the fillets with the tomato mixture.
6. Carefully, fold all the edges of to create a large packet.
7. Arrange the foil packet onto a baking sheet.
8. Bake for about 30-40 minutes or until the desired doneness of the fish.
9. Remove from the oven and serve hot.

## Tuna with Olives Sauce

**Yield:** 4 servings
**Preparation Time:** 15 minutes
**Cooking Time:** 10 minutes

**Ingredients:**

- Olive oil cooking spray
- 4 (6-ounce) (1-inch thick) tuna steaks
- 2 tablespoons extra-virgin olive oil, divided
- Salt and freshly ground black pepper, to taste
- 2 garlic cloves, minced
- 1 cup fresh tomatoes, chopped
- 1 cup dry white wine
- 2/3 cup green olives, pitted and sliced
- ¼ cup capers, drained
- 2 tablespoons fresh thyme, chopped
- 1½ tablespoons fresh lemon zest, grated
- 2 tablespoons fresh lemon juice
- 3 tablespoons fresh parsley, chopped

**Instructions:**

1. Preheat the grill to high heat. Grease the grill grate with the cooking spray.
2. Coat the tuna steaks with 1 tablespoon of the oil and sprinkle with salt and black pepper.
3. Set aside for about 5 minutes.
4. For the sauce: in a small skillet, heat the remaining oil over medium heat and sauté the garlic for about 1 minute.

5. Add the tomatoes and cook for about 2 minutes.
6. Stir in the wine and bring to a boil.
7. Add the remaining ingredients except for the parsley and cook, uncovered for about 5 minutes.
8. Stir in the parsley, salt, and black pepper and remove from the heat.
9. Meanwhile, grill the tuna steaks over direct heat for about 1-2 minutes per side.
10. Serve the tuna steaks hot with the topping of sauce.

## Tilapia with Capers

**Yield:** 4 servings
**Preparation Time:** 15 minutes
**Cooking Time:** 15 minutes

**Ingredients:**

- Olive oil cooking spray
- 1½ teaspoons paprika
- 1½ teaspoons ground cumin
- Salt and freshly ground black pepper, to taste
- 2 shallots, chopped finely
- 3 garlic cloves, minced
- 2 tablespoons fresh lemon juice
- 1½ tablespoons unsalted butter, melted
- 1 pound tilapia, cut into 8 pieces
- ¼ cup capers

**Instructions:**

1. Preheat the oven to 375 degrees F. Line a rimmed baking sheet with a parchment paper.
2. Then, grease the parchment paper with the cooking spray.
3. In a small bowl, add the paprika, cumin, salt, and black pepper and mix well.
4. In another small bowl, add the butter, shallots, garlic, lemon juice and butter, and mix until well combined.
5. Season the tilapia fillets with the spice mixture evenly and coat with the butter mixture generously.
6. Arrange the tilapia fillets onto the prepared baking sheet in a single layer and top each with the capers.
7. Bake for about 10-15 minutes or until the desired doneness of fish.
8. Remove from the oven and serve hot.

## Tilapia with Chickpeas & Veggies

**Yield:** 12 servings
**Preparation Time:** 20 minutes
**Cooking Time:** 50 minutes

**Ingredients:**

- 1 tablespoon extra-virgin olive oil
- 1 large onion, chopped
- 1 large garlic clove, chopped finely
- 1 (15-ounce) can low-sodium chickpeas, drained and rinsed
- 2 red bell peppers, seeded and cut into strips
- 1 large carrot, peeled and sliced thinly
- 3 tomatoes, chopped
- 4 olives, pitted and chopped
- ¼ cup fresh parsley, chopped
- 2 tablespoons chicken bouillon granules
- 2 tablespoons ground cumin
- 2 tablespoons paprika
- 1 teaspoon ground cayenne pepper
- Salt, to taste
- 3 pounds tilapia fillets

**Instructions:**

1. In a skillet, heat the oil over medium heat and sauté the onion and garlic for about 5 minutes.
2. Add the chickpeas, carrot, bell peppers, tomatoes and olives and cook for about 5 minutes, stirring occasionally.
3. Add the parsley, chicken bouillon granules and spices and stir to combine.

4. Arrange the tilapia fillets on top in a single layer and place enough water to cover the veggies.
5. Reduce the heat to low and simmer, covered for about 40 minutes.
6. Remove from the heat and serve hot.

### Tilapia in Herb Sauce

**Yield:** 4 servings
**Preparation Time:** 15 minutes
**Cooking Time:** 14 minutes

**Ingredients:**

- 2 (14-ounce) cans low-sodium diced tomatoes with basil and garlic, undrained
- 1/3 cup fresh parsley, chopped and divided
- ¼ teaspoon dried oregano, crushed
- ¼ teaspoon dried thyme, crushed
- ½ teaspoon red pepper flakes, crushed
- Salt and freshly ground black pepper, to taste
- 4 (6-ounce) tilapia fillets
- 2 tablespoons fresh lemon juice
- 2/3 cup feta cheese, crumbled

**Instructions:**

1. Preheat the oven to 400 degrees F.
2. In a shallow baking dish, add the tomatoes, ¼ cup of the parsley, oregano, red pepper flakes, salt, and black pepper and mix until well combined.
3. Arrange the tilapia fillets over the tomato mixture in a single layer and drizzle with the lemon juice.

4. Place some tomato mixture over the tilapia fillets and sprinkle with the feta cheese evenly.
5. Bake for about 12-14 minutes or until the desired doneness of the fish.
6. Remove from the oven and serve hot with the garnishing of remaining parsley.

## Almond Crusted Tilapia

**Yield:** 4 servings
**Preparation Time:** 15 minutes
**Cooking Time:** 10 minutes

**Ingredients:**

- 1 cup almonds, chopped finely and divided
- ¼ cup ground flax seeds
- 4 (6-ounce) tilapia fillets
- Salt and freshly ground black pepper, to taste
- 2 tablespoons olive oil

**Instructions:**

1. In a shallow bowl, add a ½ cup of the almonds and ground flax seeds and mix well.
2. Season the tilapia fillets with the salt and black pepper evenly.
3. Now, coat the tilapia fillets with the almond mixture evenly.
4. In a large heavy skillet, heat the oil over medium heat and cook the tilapia fillets for about 4 minutes per side.
5. Transfer the tilapia fillets onto a serving plate.

6. In the same skillet, add the remaining almonds and cook for about 1 minute, stirring frequently.
7. Remove the almonds from the heat and sprinkle over fish.
8. Serve warm.

### Seafood Paella

**Yield:** 4 servings
**Preparation Time:** 20 minutes
**Cooking Time:** 40 minutes

**Ingredients:**

- 1 tablespoon extra-virgin olive oil
- 1 red bell pepper, seeded and chopped finely
- 1 large yellow onion, chopped finely
- 4 garlic cloves, minced
- 1½ cups short grain rice
- ½ teaspoon ground turmeric
- 1 teaspoon paprika
- 14 ounces canned low-sodium diced tomatoes
- 2 pinches saffron threads, crushed
- 3 cups low-sodium chicken broth
- 12 mussels, cleaned
- 12 large shrimp, peeled and deveined
- ½ cup frozen peas, thawed
- ¼ cup fresh parsley, chopped
- 1 lemon, cut into wedges

**Instructions:**

1. In a deep pan, heat the oil over medium-high heat and sauté bell pepper, onion, and garlic for about 3 minutes.
2. Add the rice, turmeric, and paprika and stir to combine.
3. Stir in the tomatoes, saffron, and broth and bring to a boil.
4. Reduce the heat to low and simmer, covered for about 20 minutes.
5. Place the mussels, shrimp, and peas on top of the rice mixture and simmer, covered for about 10-15 minutes.
6. Garnish with parsley and serve hot alongside the lemon wedges.

## Rice & Veggies Jambalaya

**Yield:** 4 servings
**Preparation Time:** 20 minutes
**Cooking Time:** 55 minutes

**Ingredients:**

- 2 tablespoons olive oil
- 1 onion, chopped
- 2 celery stalks, chopped
- 4 garlic cloves, minced
- ½ of red bell pepper, seeded and chopped
- ½ of green bell pepper, seeded and chopped
- 1 (14-ounce) can low-sodium crushed tomatoes
- 2 cups uncooked brown rice

- 4 cups low-sodium vegetable broth
- 1-2 tablespoons Tabasco sauce
- 2 tablespoons low-sodium soy sauce
- 2 bay leaves
- 1 teaspoon dried thyme, crushed
- 1 teaspoon dried basil, crushed
- 1 teaspoon dried oregano, crushed
- 1 teaspoon sweet paprika
- ½ teaspoon smoked paprika
- ½ teaspoon cayenne pepper
- Freshly ground black pepper, to taste
- 3 cups low-sodium canned mixed beans (chickpeas, white beans, and kidney beans)
- Salt, to taste
- ¼ cup fresh parsley, chopped
- 1 scallion, chopped

**Instructions:**

1. In a large pan, heat the oil over medium-high heat and sauté the onion, and garlic for about 4-5 minutes or until soft.
2. Add the celery and bell peppers and sauté for about 4-5 minutes.
3. Stir in the crushed tomato, rice, broth, Tabasco sauce, soy sauce, bay leaves, dried herbs, spices, and black pepper and bring to a boil.
4. Reduce the heat to low and simmer, covered for about 30-40 minutes or until the rice is cooked and all the liquid is absorbed, stirring occasionally.
5. Uncover and stir in the beans and salt.
6. Simmer for about 2-3 minutes or until heated through.
7. Remove from the heat and serve with the garnishing of parsley and scallion.

## Quinoa & Lentil Casserole

**Yield:** 4 servings
**Preparation Time:** 15 minutes
**Cooking Time:** 48 minutes

### Ingredients:

- Olive oil cooking spray
- 2 tablespoons olive oil
- 1 large yellow onion, chopped
- 3 garlic cloves, minced
- 10 ounces fresh baby spinach
- 2½ cups cooked quinoa
- 1½ cups cooked brown lentils
- 2 cups fresh cherry tomatoes, halved
- 2 medium eggs
- ½ cup plain, non-fat Greek yogurt
- 6 ounces feta cheese, crumbled
- ½ cup fresh dill, chopped
- ½ teaspoon salt
- Pinch of freshly ground black pepper

### Instructions:

1. Preheat the oven to 375 degrees F. Grease a 9x13-inch casserole dish with the cooking spray.
2. In a large skillet, heat the oil over medium heat and sauté the onion and garlic for about 3 minutes.
3. Stir in the spinach and cook, covered for about 2½ minutes.
4. Uncover and cook for about 2½ minutes.
5. With a slotted spoon, transfer the spinach mixture onto a paper towel-lined plate to drain.

6. In a large bowl, add the quinoa, lentils, spinach mixture and tomatoes and mix.
7. In another large bowl, add the yogurt, eggs, feta, dill, salt, and black pepper and mix until well combined.
8. Add the quinoa mixture and mix until well combined.
9. Place the mixture into the prepared casserole dish evenly.
10. Bake for about 35-40 minutes or until the top becomes golden brown.
11. Remove from the oven and set aside to cool for about 10 minutes before serving.
12. Cut into desired sized slices and serve.

# Mediterranean Diet For Beginners

## 14-Day Meal Plan

### Day 1

**Breakfast:** Date & Yogurt Smoothie

**Lunch:** Grilled Prawns

**Dinner:** Spicy Lentil Soup

### Day 2

**Breakfast:** Yogurt Bowl with Caramelized Figs

**Lunch:** Chicken & Grapes Kabobs

**Dinner:** Cannellini Beans & Farro Stew

### Day 3

**Breakfast:** Spiced Quinoa Porridge

**Lunch:** Pasta with Mushrooms

**Dinner:** Bruschetta Chicken Breasts

**Day 4**

**Breakfast:** Oat Pancakes

**Lunch:** Mussels in Wine & Tomato Sauce

**Dinner:** Quinoa & Vegetables Stew

**Day 5**

**Breakfast:** Eggs in spicy Veggie Sauce

**Lunch:** Beef & Veggie Pizza

**Dinner:** Seafood Paella

**Day 6**

**Breakfast:** Strawberry & Yogurt Muffins

**Lunch:** Zucchini & Basil Soup

**Dinner:** Chicken Breasts with Balsamic Fig Sauce

**Day 7**

**Breakfast:** Veggies & Egg Scramble

**Lunch:** Rigatoni with Salmon

**Dinner:** Beef & Prunes Stew


**Day 8**

**Breakfast:** Overnight Oatmeal with Figs

**Lunch:** Tabbouleh

**Dinner:** Steak with Yogurt Sauce


**Day 9**

**Breakfast:** Honeyed Ricotta & Pear Toast

**Lunch:** Chickpeas Stew

**Dinner:** Veggies & Feta Stuffed Leg of Lamb


**Day 10**

**Breakfast:** Baked Yogurt Crepes

**Lunch:** Vegetables Curry

**Dinner:** Baked Fish with Tomatoes & Capers

**Day 11**

**Breakfast:** Strawberry Smoothie Bowl

**Lunch:** Lamb Filled Pita with Yogurt Sauce

**Dinner:** Baked Fish with Tomatoes & Capers


**Day 12**

**Breakfast:** Tomato Omelet

**Lunch:** Orzo & Veggie Salad

**Dinner:** Tilapia in Herb Sauce


**Day 13**

**Breakfast:** Mixed Veggies Smoothie

**Lunch:** Lamb Koftas with Yogurt Sauce

**Dinner:** Halibut Parcel


**Day 14**

**Breakfast:** Veggies & Chickpeas Hash

**Lunch:** Chicken Sandwich with Aioli

**Dinner:** Rice & Veggies Jambalaya

## Healthy Tips for Home Cooking

At this day and age, our busy schedules leave us to nothing but the Drive-thru or take away. But to your surprise, home cooking has never been easier if planned well. Moreover, there are plenty of helpful kitchen gadgets that have made home cooking even easier. The only thing you need is to be well-organized. Undoubtedly, home cooking is the best and smartest way to slim down and shed those extra pounds. Here are some of the tips to help you organize well and get benefitted from cooking at home?

1. Choose a proper meal plan for the whole week.
2. Make a shopping list over the weekend for coming a week and shop all you need for the meals you're making a coming week.
3. Don't forget to fill up your pantry with healthy foods only. That is, to avoid junk and collect healthy snacks.
4. If you are a working person, use meal prep tips.
5. Use helpful kitchen gadgets like Pressure cookers, air fryers, etc to make it quicker and healthier.

**Essential Principles for Weight Loss**

Out of many, these are the most essential weight loss principles that you have to stick to in order to achieve a healthier and more permanent weight loss.

1. On top of the list, prepare yourself to accept the changes.
2. Create a long-term strategy that will help you with weight loss.
3. Set the goals to follow the weight loss plan strictly.
4. Get a variety of foods in moderation in your menu list so you don't get bored quickly.
5. Drink plenty of water daily.
6. Exercise regularly.
7. Avoid artificial sweeteners or fizzy drinks.
8. If you are using canned food, then make sure to buy low-sodium and low-fat products.
9. Last but not least, Be Persistent!

*P.S: Thanks for reading: if you enjoyed this book, please consider leaving an short review on Amazon.*

## Conclusion

The Mediterranean diet is based upon the cuisines and culture of the Mediterranean region. Numerous scientific and medical studies have argued and proven that the Mediterranean diet is very healthy and is a perfect diet plan for avoiding various chronic diseases like cancer, cardiac complications and also for boosting life expectancy. The Mediterranean diet is very different in its fat intake from the rest of the diet plans. Mediterranean cuisine involves higher content of unsaturated fat like olive oil and lower content of saturated fats. Saturated fats are mainly present in dairy products and meat apart from their slight presence in a few nuts, avocados and certain vegetable oils.

Numerous well-known scientific studies claim that the risk of heart-related complications and diseases can be lowered by increasing the intake of a type of dietary fat i.e. the mono-saturated fat, which is present mostly in olive oils. This argument of Studies has concluded that unsaturated fats have been credited with a high amount of HDL cholesterol which is also referred to as "the good" cholesterol. The reason for HDL cholesterol being credited as a friend for the body is that protects the body from cardiovascular complications.

Made in the USA
Middletown, DE
27 August 2019